Spells
for the
Solitary
Witch

Spells for the Solitary Witch

Eileen Holland

WEISER BOOKS
Boston, MA/York Beach, ME

First published in 2004 by
Red Wheel/Weiser, LLC
York Beach, ME
With offices at:
368 Congress Street
Boston, MA 02210
www.redwheelweiser.com

Library of Congress Cataloging-in-Publication Data

Holland, Eileen.
  Spells for the solitary witch / Eileen Holland.
      p. cm.
  Includes index.
   ISBN 1-57863-294-3
   1. Witchcraft. 2. Magic. I. Title.
   BF1566.H643 2004
   133.4'4--dc22

                              2003025441

Typeset in ITC Giovanni and Clairvaux

Printed in Canada
TCP
11 10 09 08 07 06 05 04
  8 7 6 5 4 3 2

*This book is dedicated to all those who serve Isis,
Great Magician, Lady of Spells, Lady of Words of
Power, Goddess of Many Names, Queen of the
Universe, Mistress of All Things Forever.*

Contents

Before You Begin

Solitary witches are those who practice the Craft without a coven or other group. Some witches are solitary because of circumstances, but the rest of us are solitary by choice. We enjoy gathering with other witches for sabbats, festivals, or rituals, and we sometimes participate in group spells or other concerted magickal actions, but we feel no need to join a formal group. We understand that there is a difference between being alone and being lonely. We like our independence and prefer the freedom to do things our own way.

This book's spells are all designed to be cast by a single witch, working alone. Coveners can also use them, when they work by themselves or by adapting the spells for group use.

Love, money, wishes, uncrossing, protection . . . whatever your need, there is likely to be a spell for it here. Candle magick, knot magick, footprint magick, sympathetic magick, herbal magick, psi-magick, talismanic magick, kitchen witchcraft . . . there are many different kinds of spells in the book. Smudging, asperging, invocation, incantation, visualization . . . many different magickal techniques are used. Charms, potions, poppets, mojo bags, spell bottles, rituals . . . whatever your skill level, there is something here for you.

If you are an experienced witch (or otherwise adept at magick), cast these spells in your usual way. You can also adapt them as needed or use them to inspire creation of your own spells and rituals.

New Practitioners

If you are new to magick, it is very important that you read this entire section before you cast the spells. Here are some of the things that you need to know: Magick is serious. Magick is subtle. Magick is sacred. Magick is spiritual. Magick is science. Magick is love. Magick flows from the Goddess. Magick is the manipulation of energy. Magick is all around us, if we know how to perceive it.

Many of this book's readers will be new to magick, and I have kept them in mind while writing it. Casting a magick circle can be daunting for new practitioners, so these spells can all be worked without circles. (If you usually cast circles for your spells, though, by all means please do so for these as well.)

How do you create spells for people who have little experience with magick—spells they can actually make work? My solution has been to base most of these on correspondences and invocation. Everything in them, from ingredients to timing to deities, is specified because it empowers the spell's intent.

Correspondences and Invocation

Magick teaches us that everything in the Universe is connected. Correspondences are magickal associations. They link herbs, animals, crystals, colors, lunar phases, and so on with specific energies, and thus with intended magickal results. Correspondences are powerful keys that help to open specific doors, and thereby direct magickal energy in desired ways.

If you have prior knowledge of magick, you will understand why certain herbs, candle colors, and so on are used in the spells, and why it is recommended that some spells be cast on particular days or during specified phases of the Moon. If you have no understanding of these things, you can nonetheless make use of magickal correspondences by simply following the directions for the spells in this book.

Names of deities are ancient Words of Power, so we invoke gods and goddesses to boost the magickal power of our spells. Different deities have dominion over different things, so we invoke them in accord with the intent of our spells. If you have studied mythology, you will understand why this god or that goddess is called upon in a spell. If you know nothing about mythology, you can still access of the power of invocation by following the spell directions.

A glossary of deity names is provided at the end of the book. It gives a very basic outline of who these gods and goddesses are.

Intent and Intensity

These are cornerstones of magick, because no spell can be cast without them. A spell's purpose, or intent, is what that spell is meant to accomplish. A spell will not work properly unless you are very clear, in your mind and in your words, about what you mean the spell to do. Focused intent is crucial in spell-work, so many of this book's spells use writing as a technique to help with that.

Intensity is the power, passion, and energy that you pour into casting a spell. If you are ambivalent or uncertain about a spell, it is not likely to be fulfilled. The more intensity you put into it, the more successful that spell is likely to be. Keep this in mind when you raise power.

Belief, Respect, Ethics, and Responsibility

Magick cannot be practiced successfully without belief, respect, ethics, and responsibility. If you do not believe in magick, you will not be able to make magick. If you do not believe in yourself, and in your ability to work magick, you will not be able to make magick work for you. If you do not believe that you deserve the blessings that magick can bring, you will not be able to accept blessings—even when they make themselves available to you. It is possible to faithfully follow the instructions for these or other spells and still not have them work. You have to believe in magick, believe in yourself, and believe in your ability in order to work magick successfully.

It is dangerous to attempt to use magick unless you have respect for it. Failure to respect magick can result in having your spells go horribly wrong. To prevent this from happening, you must respect yourself, respect others, and respect the elements and the Universe, as well as respecting magick.

Magick does not work well for people who doubt themselves or have low self-esteem. If that sounds like you, work on those issues before you try to cast spells. Do whatever inner work is needed to get to really know yourself, to like and appreciate yourself, before you try to cast spells. Self-respect gives you the confidence you need to have in order to get spells to work.

To meddle magickally in someone's life is to disrespect that person. No matter how good or honorable our intentions may be, we should not cast spells for people unless they ask us for magickal help. To do otherwise is to invite interference in our own lives and affairs.

Successful magick requires a healthy respect for the elements (Earth, Air, Fire, Water). This is especially true of Fire. If you leave candles, incense, or anything else burning unattended, you will learn this lesson the hard way.

Respect the Universe by living an honest, ethical, useful life. Be a good citizen of the Universe. Try to be of service to others, instead of focusing solely on yourself and your needs. Protect children, animals, and all who cannot protect themselves. Be a producer as well as a consumer, and do what you can to help Mother Nature.

We were given a gorgeous planet, but its precious natural resources are dwindling because of human use, abuse, and overuse. Acknowledge that fact. Respect it by trying to live gently upon the Earth. Recycle. Be kind to creatures. Make ethical choices. Educate yourself about the environment. Consider it when you buy a car or do anything else that affects the environment. Everything is connected, so the kind of life you live influences your ability to work magick. If you respect the Universe, you will find it more responsive to you than if you did not respect it.

Use magick judiciously. Don't cast spells for every little problem or issue. Try ordinary solutions first. Don't disturb the gods unless it's important. Be responsible for yourself, instead of expecting them to solve your problems for you. Try to serve magick instead of asking it to serve you. If you respect magick, it will respect you.

What goes around, comes around. This means that when we work magick that is kind, positive, and beneficial, blessings will be returned to us. It also means that if we work magick that is negative, mean-spirited, or harmful, it will rebound upon us in unpleasant ways sooner or later.

Spells are powerful. They can do great good, but they can also do great harm. Spells cast in anger, envy, hatred, or any other negative frame of mind are more likely to backfire than they are to work as intended. Ethics provide a framework in which to safely practice magick. Keep that in mind, and your spells will not hurt you.

To work magick successfully, you must be responsible for yourself and your actions. This includes accepting responsibility for the results of your spells. Approaching magick with this in mind helps to keep us on the right path. It prevents us from casting spells that we later regret.

To rely on magick alone would be unrealistic and irresponsible. If you cast a spell to find a job, for example, you must also list yourself with employment agencies, send out résumés, go on interviews, and take other appropriate nonmagickal actions. If you do not take those steps, even the best job spell has very little chance of working. We help our spells to succeed by taking concrete real-world actions to support them.

Terminology

These are terms you need to know in order to follow the instructions for the spells in this book.

asperging: This is the ritual sprinkling of a liquid, such as holy water.

balancing: To balance yourself is to achieve a state of equilibrium, to be in sync with yourself and with the world. It also means to be whole, to be sane, and to integrate all aspects of yourself, such as your dark and light sides or male and female selves.

cardinal points: These are the four directions: North, South, East, and West.

centering: To center is to gather yourself, to connect completely with your inner self. To be centered means to be alert, attentive, focused, and very much present in the here and now.

chakra: An energy node in the human body.

deosil, widdershins: In the Northern Hemisphere, deosil means clockwise (to the right), and widdershins means counterclockwise (to the left). This meaning is reversed in the Southern Hemisphere.

energy signature: This is the unique energy field of a person, animal, plant, rock, or inanimate object.

grounding; grounding power: The term "ground" has two meanings in the Craft. To ground yourself means to break a magickal mood and return to ordinary consciousness.

To ground power means to return the energy that you have raised for a spell, to send it back to its source. One simple way to do this is to shake your hands, palms down, over the floor or earth. Power should always be returned after a spell. Keeping power is never a good idea. The least of its dangers is that it can cause unpleasant things such as angry spirits or malevolent entities to enter your life.

In a nonmagickal context, to be grounded means to be firmly in touch with reality. To ground yourself means to climb down from cloud nine and get real.

magick circle: A magick circle is actually a sphere, a ball of energy created to encapsulate sacred space and facilitate the casting of a spell. Witches cast magick circles around themselves and their altars in order to amplify the power raised for a spell. They are dissolved afterward, when grounding power. Magick circles are created within the square (actually a cube) formed by the cardinal points.

magickal mood: This isn't a technical term, it's just my expression for the shift in consciousness and state of heightened awareness that are a necessary prelude to working magick. Music, incense, chanting, drumming, and ritual garb, make-up, or masks are some of the triggers that practitioners use to reach this state. Whatever works for you, feel free to incorporate it with these spells when you cast them.

power animal: This is an animal (real or symbolic) with whom a practitioner has a special relationship; it is an animal that is called upon for protection, guidance, or assistance. Wolves, cats, ravens, and dragons are popular power animals.

projective hand, receptive hand: Your projective hand is the one you most often use for writing. Your receptive hand is the one you do not usually write with. If you are ambidextrous, you must decide which of your hands

feels more powerful to you and use that as your
projective hand.

psi-magick: This is magick that is worked solely with the
mind, without using candles, crystals, incense, tools, or
anything else. Many practitioners consider it the most
advanced form of magick.

raising power: This is to gather energy for the purpose of
working magick. Energy flows all around us: solar power,
wind power, water power, bio-energy, storm power, and
so on. We can tap into any power source when we want
to cast a spell.

　　Here is one simple way that you can learn to do it:
Go to a place with an abundance of natural energy, such
as the ocean, a windmill, a herd of animals, a waterfall,
or a mighty river. Approach the power source,
maintaining a safe distance. If you are using a storm,
wait for it to approach you (while you stay safely
indoors). Close your eyes and use all of your other
senses to experience the power that the source emits.
When you feel that your mind and/or body holds the
signature of the power source, and you are sure that you
will clearly remember this sensation, open your eyes.

　　Use your mind to experiment with channeling that
power through your body. Repeat this experience as many
times as you need, until you understand how to raise
power. Keep working at it, and there will come a time
when you no longer need to be in the presence of a power
source in order to make your body a conduit for power.

runes: This is an ancient Norse alphabet that is used for
magick and divination.

sabbats: These are the eight annual religious festivals
celebrated by witches: Yule (Winter Solstice), Imbolc

(February 2), Ostara (Spring Equinox), Beltane (May 1),
~~June~~Midsummer (Summer Solstice), Lughnasadh (August 1),
~~21~~ Mabon (Autumn Equinox) and Samhain (October 31).
Sept 20

sacred space: This is any area that has been cleared for
magick, ritual, meditation, or worship. It can be created
in many different ways. The clearing and sanctifying of a
space can be done physically by asperging it, sweeping it
out with a besom, or smudging it with incense. Some
practitioners create sacred space by ringing bells, lighting
candles, sounding gongs, drumming, or playing music.

  Sacred space can also be created with the mind, by
mentally defining an area and declaring it sacred for the
duration of its dedicated use. You should create sacred
space in whatever way is comfortable for you.
Visualization can be helpful with this—picture a
glowing light surrounding the space or a mist filling it.
You should create sacred space in whatever way is
comfortable for you.

scrying: This is divination by means of gazing into
something reflective, such as pooled water or a dark
mirror, until images can be seen. Cauldrons are
traditional vessels for this. It generally takes a lot of
patience and practice to become good at scrying.

smudging: This means to treat with smoke. Smudge pots are
used in agriculture to protect crops or orchards against
frost or insects. Incense is used for smudging in the
Craft, for magickal operations such as clearing,
consecrating, averting, and protecting.

spirit of place: Pleasant, unpleasant, or neutral, spirit of
place is the energy signature of a location.

third eye: Your third eye is your brow chakra, located in your forehead.

totem animal: This is an animal that symbolizes a person or a group. A tribe or clan or coven, for example, can be represented by a horse, raven, butterfly, or some other animal.

Spell Ingredients

If someone came to my door and asked to borrow a cup of yarrow, some mugwort, or African juju powder, I could accommodate the request. That is not the case with most people, though, so forget about wolfbane, witch grass, Solomon's seal, and mandrake roots. This book's spells require ordinary ingredients. Most of them can be found in supermarkets, or are things that you are likely to already have in your home.

If you know your correspondences and want to substitute more esoteric ingredients for those called for here, go right ahead. Unless otherwise indicated in a spell, the substitutions given below may also be used.

altar: If you do not have an altar, or if your altar is not suitable for casting spells, a flat surface such as a table, desk, or counter can be substituted.

besom: This is a witch's broom, one that is reserved for magick and ritual. A besom can look like an ordinary broom, or it can be handmade or elaborately decorated. Any brand-new, unused broom can be substituted for a besom.

candles: It is understood that when this book's spells call for candles, that means candles in appropriate holders that will allow them to burn safely. If a spell requires a candle to be burned atop anything, the holder should be one that will catch any wax that may drip from the candle.

Be mindful of fire safety in deciding where and how to burn candles, and supervise them while they burn. It doesn't matter if you use an elaborate silver candelabrum or saucers from the kitchen; what matters is that you burn your candles without causing harm to anyone or anything. Unless you have a lot of time to monitor them, it's best to use small candles such as votives or short tapers for spells.

White candles can be substituted for candles of any other color. When a black candle is called for, a white candle can be burned upside-down in its place.

carving tools: For the purposes of this book, a carving tool means something that will cut into wax—something you can use to inscribe a candle. You can use a white-handled knife or something elaborate if you like, but the tip of a ballpoint pen will usually suffice for carving candles.

combustion: It is understood that every spell that calls for incense or candles will also require a way to light them. Use matches, lighters, an altar candle, or whatever you like for this.

herbs: Rosemary is powerful and has many magickal attributes, so it can be substituted for almost any other herbs in spells.

incense: It is understood that when this book's spells call for incense, that means incense in a holder that will allow it to burn safely. It doesn't matter if you burn an exotic resin in a fancy censer or if you poke an incense stick into the dirt of a potted plant; what matters is that you burn your incense without causing harm to anything or anyone. Be mindful of fire safety in deciding where and how to burn incense, and monitor it while it burns.

Sandalwood incense is so universal that it can be

SPELLS FOR THE SOLITARY WITCH

substituted for any other incense in spells. If you are experienced enough with resin or loose incense to safely burn it over self-igniting charcoal disks, this is the best method to use. If you have incense sticks or cones or prefer to smolder an essential oil over an oil burner, that's fine.

mojo bags: "Mojo" means magick. A mojo bag is a small bag with a drawstring at the top, such as the little velveteen bags in which jewelry and perfume samples are sometimes packaged. Mojo bags can be purchased, or made from any fabric in any color. For magick it makes little difference how elaborate or well-made a mojo bag is; even a square of cloth that is tied into a bundle could serve as a mojo bag. Neutral-color bags, such as white, beige, and gray, can be substituted for any color mojo bag.

pentagram, pentacle: A pentagram is a two-dimensional representation of a five-pointed star in a circle. Unless a spell calls for it to be reversed, a pentagram should always be positioned this way: ⊛ . A pentacle is a three-dimensional representation of the same symbol—for instance, on a ring, trivet, or pendant.

poppet: A poppet is something that represents a human being, such as a cloth figure.

stones: Crystals and other stones can be used in more than one spell, if you clear them after each working. Clearing is important because using a crystal that retains vibrations from a previous spell can interfere with the outcome of a new spell. Water, salt, incense, sunlight, and moonlight can all be used, alone or in combination, to clear stones. For example, you might wash a crystal in running water, place it in a dish of salt, and then put the dish in sunlight for a period of time. The more clearing that you feel the stone needs, the longer you leave it in the dish. You might instead smudge a stone with incense, then place it overnight in moonlight to clear it. You can clear stones in whatever way you like. The important thing is that you feel that a stone has been cleared of any magickal residue before you use it in another spell.

Because they can most easily be programmed and reprogrammed, clear quartz crystals can be substituted for almost any stone in any spell. One way to do this is to take the crystal, hold it in sunlight or moonlight, say:

"Crystal, for this spell you are given the powers of _____," and name the stone whose energies are required. After the spell has been cast, clear the crystal to restore it to its original state.

Timing

Casting spells in accordance with Moon phases increases their potency. To do this you can observe the skies every night, as our remote ancestors did, or you can get a calendar that has the Moon phases on it. (Most of us opt for the calendar.) Full Moon is when the Moon can be seen as a complete circle. Waning Moon means the period between Full Moon and New Moon, when the Moon appears to be growing smaller. Waxing Moon is the period between New Moon and Full Moon, when the Moon appears to be growing larger.

Astrological timing is also used to increase the power of spells. Look to almanacs, especially magickal and astrological almanacs, for information about which planets the Sun and Moon are in at any given time. The days of the week have magickal correspondences as well, such as Sun-day for solar power, so that is reflected in some of the spells given here.

꙳

As you work with magick it becomes more and more clear that everything truly is connected. Energy may be invisible, but it is still perceivable. If you are attentive when you hold stones or work with herbs, you will notice that different kinds have different vibrations. If you are cognizant of lunar phases or the positions of planets you will notice their effect on you, on others, and on current events. If you pay close attention to such things, you learn to appreciate the subtle energies that flow through and around us. Spells are tools for influencing these energies to effect desired results.

Spells
for the
Solitary
Witch

~1~

Inner Work

Inner work empowers us. It helps us to understand ourselves, streamline our lives, and progress along our individual paths. By teaching us to awaken, recognize, and appreciate our abilities, inner work stills our doubts in ourselves. This helps us to work magick.

It is through inner work that we achieve our full potential, and spells in this chapter can help you with that.

~ Open Sesame Third Eye Spell ~

This is a joyful spell, so if you feel moved to dance, chant, whirl, or sing while casting it, by all means please do so. If you are new to magick or to psychic work, or find that your psychic abilities aren't as sharp as they once were, this is a good spell for you.

Your third eye is the center of your psychic self. Your sixth chakra, it rules every aspect of your sixth sense: intuition, insight, clairvoyance, precognition, telepathy, and all other psychic abilities. Your third eye helps you to see the unseen, and to perceive more than is possible with your ordinary senses.

Opening your third eye (or activating your sixth chakra, if you prefer that term) is an important prelude to psychic work. This includes everything from meditation, divination, visualization, scrying, crystallomancy, and fire-gazing to distance healing, past-life work, dream work, remote viewing, astral projection, and so on.

This spell may be cast at any time, but it is best cast on a moonlit night. You will need:

+ sandalwood incense

+ a purple candle

+ sesame oil (You can find edible sesame oil where Asian food products are sold, and scented sesame oil is sold with skin care products.)

+ Tiger Balm (This is a liniment that is used for headaches and muscle pain. Packaged in tiny jars, it can be found in health food shops, at some pharmacies, and in stores that sell Asian products. Tiger Balm contains ingredients that make the skin tingle, such as menthol. Its use in this spell is to make you more aware of your third eye, so you could substitute anything that will make your skin tingle, such as another commercial liniment, essential oil of peppermint, or whatever your ingenuity devises. Use anything you like, but be sure it's something that seems magickal to you and to which your skin is not allergic.)

+ *Optional*: music, ritual garb, or whatever helps you to get into a magickal mood. (You could use any music that appeals to you, but if you are fortunate enough to own a recording of the late great Egyptian diva Om Kalsoum singing "Alfy Layla wa Layla" [A Thousand and One Nights], that would make an especially powerful accompaniment.)

Preparation

Some traditions consider the third eye to be located between the eyebrows, while others consider it located in the middle of the forehead. We are all different, so only you can determine the location of your third eye. If you aren't sure, get a small crystal and place it between your eyebrows. Does it tingle, in a psychic way? If not, place the crystal in the center of your forehead. How does that feel? It may take repeated tries if you are new to all of this, but you will eventually find a spot on your forehead that responds to the presence of the crystal. When you do, that is the location of your third eye.

Dress the candle with the sesame oil, by using the forefinger of your projective hand to rub the candle with it. Wash your hands.

The Spell

Open the jar of Tiger Balm, and put it on your altar or other working surface with the candle and the incense. Get into a magickal mood, and create sacred space. Darken the room. Light the candle, then light the incense from the candle. Anoint your third eye with the Tiger Balm, again using the forefinger of your projective hand. Raise power.

Focus on the way that your third eye is responding to the Tiger Balm and to the warmth of the candle. Concentrate on opening your third eye. Do this by visualizing it unfolding as a flower does when it blooms. Gaze at the candle until you feel ready, then say:

> *Alfy layla wa layla,*[1]
> *Alfy layla wa layla . . .*
> *By the Moon, on Arabian nights,*
> *By the silence of ancient sites,*

---

1. Translation Note: *alfy layla wa layla* is Arabic for "one thousand and one nights"; *ifta, ya simsim* is Arabic for "open sesame."

Pronunciation Note: Both phrases have been rendered in English exactly as they sound in Egyptian-dialect Arabic.

By the secrets of arcane rites,
By the flicker of candle lights . . .
Ifta, ya simsim!
Open sesame!
Open my third eye, open my mind's eye,
Release my sixth sense.
Help me to see the unseen.
Let me Be as I have never been,

Let me See as I have never seen.
Open my third eye, open my mind's eye,
Open my Self to understanding.
alfy layla wa layla
alfy layla wa layla . . .
By the power of moonlight,
By the power of clear sight,
Ifta, ya simsim!
Open sesame!

Concentrate on your third eye, now wide open. Envision stars pouring from the chakra, or light pouring into it, or whatever image feels right to you. If you have been blocked for a long time, or if you raised a lot of power for this spell, a tremendous amount of energy may be released. Don't be frightened if this causes a physical manifestation, such as the candle flame suddenly leaping up. Don't be concerned if your body begins to vibrate or if the energy affects you in some other physical way. Dance, if this happens and you feel that you need to work the energy off.

Gaze into the flame of the candle. Concentrate on how you feel and on the possibilities that the spell has released. Do this until you feel your body adjust itself to the now open chakra, then begin to ground the power that you raised. Monitor the candle until it has burned down entirely. You should feel calm, grounded, and centered by then. Ground any residual power, and clean up. Have something to eat and drink if you have trouble returning to ordinary consciousness.

Afterward

You will be changed after you cast this spell. It will affect different people differently. You may find that you are more imaginative, that your perception is keener, your meditations deeper, or your insight sharper. You might find visualization easier or begin to get more accurate answers from your runes, pendulum, tarot cards, or whatever divination tool you regularly use.

Opening your third eye can also affect your body. You may find yourself sleeping better, feeling less anxious, less confused, or less fearful. You might begin to experience fewer or less severe headaches. You could also feel less tension in your neck, or have eye, hormone, or skin problems finally clear up.

However this spell affects you, it will be a positive change. Some will cast it once and have their third eye forever opened. Others will find it helpful to cast the spell periodically in order to keep their third eye open.

⚬ Spirit of Acceptance Spell ⚬

We human beings have a remarkable talent for sabotaging ourselves. We excel at creating our own problems, at erecting roadblocks and detours along our paths, and at stubbornly refusing to act in our own best interests. Sometimes these issues relate to our failure or refusal to accept things, such as the truth about ourselves, the truth about people and situations, changes that need to be made, the reality of our circumstances, or the blessings that the Universe offers us.

Use this spell if you think that you are having problems with acceptance. It can be cast at any time but is best cast while the Moon is waxing (the period between New Moon and Full Moon—use a calendar to time it). You will need:

- ✦ a mojo bag
- ✦ enough mustard seeds to fill one-third of the bag (Get these where spices are sold.)
- ✦ a small crystal
- ✦ a piece of good paper
- ✦ a pen (Don't use a pencil because you want the spell to last.)
- ✦ two sticks of incense, in any scent you like
- ✦ *Optional*: a sprig of fresh clover
- ✦ *Optional*: music, candles, ritual garb, or whatever helps you to alter your consciousness

Preparation

Get into a magickal mood. Assemble all of the spell ingredients on your altar or other working surface. Light a stick of incense, and create sacred space around the area where you will be working. Put the mustard seeds and the crystal into the mojo bag. Smudge the bag by holding it in the incense smoke and turning it until the entire bag has been touched by the smoke.

The Spell

Tear the paper into thin strips. On the first one write, "I accept myself." Fold or roll it tightly, and put it into the bag. On the next two strips write, "I accept responsibility for myself and my actions" and "I accept responsibility for my life." On a fourth strip write, "I accept that I deserve the blessings of this Universe." Fold or roll the paper strips and put them into the mojo bag.

Using as many more strips of paper as necessary, write down all of the other things that you want or need to accept. Depending on your issues, this might include things such as, "I accept reality"; "I accept change"; "I accept my body"; "I accept my illness"; "I accept compromise"; "I accept my family"; "I accept healing"; "I accept my past"; "I accept recovery"; "I accept my success"; "I accept my losses"; "I accept adulthood"; "I accept love into my life"; "I accept that death is a necessary part of the spiral of life"; "I accept that I need to make positive changes in my life"; "I accept transformation"; or whatever the case may be. If you worry that you might have overlooked something, write "I accept everything that I need to accept."

Take your time, and give this careful thought. It's your life, so you are probably the only one who really knows what you need. Be honest, be thorough, and fold or roll the strips of paper tightly so that they will all fit into the mojo bag. If it seems as though you will run out of room, write on both sides of the strips.

If you have a sprig of clover, add it to the bag after the final strip of paper. Light the second stick of incense. Pull the drawstrings to close the mojo bag, and knot them over the top. Tie three knots, if possible. Raise power, and hold the bag in the smoke as you say:

> *Crafted so it does no harm,*
> *With magick I enchant this charm.*
> *Winds of change, blow through me.*
> *Spirit of acceptance, flow to me.*
> *This I command, so mote it be!*

Hold the bag in the smoke until the incense burns completely down, repeating the spell as many times as you feel is needed. Ground power once the incense is spent, and clean up the work space. Discard the candle, the remains of the incense, and any unused spell ingredients.

Keep the mojo bag with you until the spell has fully manifested. Place it near your bed or under your pillow while you sleep, and wear or carry it during the day. This spell will provide gradual results that will snowball once they get going. It will help you to begin to feel better about yourself and about your life. Remember that transformation is a process rather than a quick change, even if a sudden event sparked the transformation.

Afterward

You can renew this spell at any time by holding the mojo bag in incense smoke and repeating the words of the spell.

When the issues that brought you to needing this spell are no longer issues, you can consider the spell's work complete. The mojo bag can then be buried, burned, thrown out, put away in a safe place, or disposed of in whatever way seems best to you. The crystal may be cleared (see "stones" under "Spell Ingredients" on page xviii for instructions on how to do this) and retained for future use, if you like.

Release Spells

Are you carrying a torch, holding a grudge, or nursing an emotional wound? Do you harbor negative emotions such as anger, bitterness, regret, resentment, or recrimination? Do you ache with fear, sorrow, tension, or anxiety? Do you labor under false illusions, repeat negative patterns, or have unhealthy attachments? Do you accept abuse, enable restrictions, or ignore truth while you buy into falsehoods? If so, these spells can help you.

We all have baggage of one sort or another, negative people, habits, thoughts, or patterns that we accumulate as we travel down the roads of our lives. It is helpful to periodically let go of the things that weigh us down and prevent us from getting on with life.

Look deep within yourself. Look into your mind, your heart, your memory, your personality, your life, and your spirit. What are your issues? Be honest with yourself. Meditation is a tool that can help us to identify what we would be better off without. Once you have defined your issues, you are ready for these spells.

⊹ Bursting Bubbles Spell ⊱

This spell can be cast at any time. Use caution, as always, when working with fire. You will need:

+ a pen (Use one with with green or purple ink, if possible.)

+ a piece of white paper

+ a green or purple candle

+ a fireproof container

+ a stick of incense (If possible, use cedar, copal, dragon's blood, frankincense, myrrh, patchouli, or sandalwood.)

+ a sheet of bubble wrap (Bubble wrap can be found in office supply stores and where packing and shipping supplies are sold. You could even use a sheet that came wrapped around something you purchased.)

+ a vessel of water for fire safety

Preparation

Identify all the personal issues that you need to release, and write them down. Take your time with this, in order to be thorough. It's fine if you take days, or even weeks, to accomplish this part of the spell. As you write, phrase your issues in this manner: my bitterness, my envy, my anger, my pessimism, my unrealistic optimism, my feelings of guilt, my tendency to blame others, my tendency to blame myself for things that are not my fault, or whatever may apply in your case.

When your list is complete, count the number of items on it. You will need one bubble for each item, so be sure that you have enough bubble wrap for this. Trim the sheet until it has exactly the required number of bubbles. If you have more items than bubbles on the sheet, use a second sheet and trim that one as needed.

The Spell

Gather the spell materials. Put the fireproof container on your altar or other working surface on something that will not scorch if its bottom gets hot. Put the water near it, and open a window.

Light the candle, then light the incense from the candle. Get into a magickal mood, and create sacred space around the area where you will be working. Read your list (aloud or in your mind), focusing on each item for a few moments. Imagine each issue as a dark bubble in your spirit. Picture the dark bubbles swirling chaotically inside you, and concentrate on your desire to be rid of them.

Raise power. Visualize the bubbles quieting down and lining up for departure. Pick up the bubble wrap. Work your way through the list, saying for each item:

I release _____. Go forth.
Do no harm, and never return to me.

As you say this, pop one bubble on the wrap. Visualize that dark bubble leaving you to burst harmlessly in the air over the incense or the candle. Picture the bubble's energy being carried away with the smoke. Continue this way until you have finished your list. You should feel relieved, feel lightened, and be energized by this process.

As you did in childhood, fold the paper into a fan. Use it to waft the smoke toward the open window. Visualize everything that you have released floating out of the window and away from you. When you feel that this has been done, touch the paper to the candle flame and drop it, blazing, into the fireproof container.

Remain there until everything has finished burning, then ground power and clean up.

⁖ "Get Over It" Spell ⁖

Whether your burden is a failed relationship, a difficult childhood, a financial loss, a crime, an unrealized dream, or something else, you can use this spell to help yourself finally get over it. The god Saturn has dominion over endings that lead to new beginnings, so this spell is best cast on a Saturday (Saturn's day). You will need:

+ a stick of incense (Any kind will do, but use fumitory if you are fortunate enough to find it.)
+ a sheet of paper
+ a black pen
+ a piece of black thread or ribbon
+ a trowel or small shovel

Preparation

Identify your problem, and use the black pen to write it on the paper. Write it as succinctly as possible, in a word or short phrase such as: my marriage, the fire, my childhood, the robbery, the accident, the affair, the war, a person's name, or whatever your personal issue is. If you have more than one matter to get over, write them all down.

The Spell

Get into a magickal mood, and create sacred space around the area where you will be working. Light the incense, and raise power. Spend a few minutes looking at what you have written on the paper. Focus on the fact that these words, and the events or people they represent, are no longer a part of you. Roll the paper into a cylinder, and waft it through the incense smoke. As you do this, say aloud:

Smoke curl, paper furl,
By the power of fumitory,
I expel you from my thoughts.
You have no power over me.

Repeat this as many times as feel necessary to you, and believe it when you say it.

Next, crumple the paper into a ball. Place it in a doorway, so that it will be caught between the door and its frame when the door closes. Slam the door on the paper, and say aloud,

Door jamb, door slam,
By the power of Janus,
I shut the door on _____.
This chapter of my life is closed!

Use the words that you wrote on your paper to fill in the blank at the end of that sentence. If slamming the door repeatedly on the paper would help you to release pent-up emotions, go ahead and do it.

Remove the ball of paper from the doorway. Tear it into long strips (or run it through a paper shredder). Gather the strips into a bundle, and tie it with the black thread or ribbon. Fold the strips as many times as possible, tying them with the thread each time. The incense should have finished burning by then, and you should have a small package of paper and thread that represents the issue(s) you intend to get over.

Ground the power that you raised. Toss the bundle in a corner or near the trash to show yourself how little it now means to you. Clean up. You could complete this spell immediately, or you could complete it early the next morning. That is the best choice, because dawn is an auspicious time for fresh starts and bright beginnings.

To conclude the spell, retrieve the bundled strips of paper, and get the trowel. Take them outside, and bury the package in a place where you frequently walk, such as in your yard or driveway. Be sure to bury it deeply enough that it is not likely to be unearthed by rain, animals, or anything else.

If you cannot bury the paper, perhaps because you live in a city where all ground surfaces are paved, or because it's winter and the earth is frozen solid, use your ingenuity to find a way to complete the spell. One way to do it, provided your plumbing can handle it, is to flush the bundle down the toilet.

Afterward

Whenever you come to the place where you buried the bundle, stand on it and say, "I am over it." Take a step past it and say, "It is behind me." Take another step and say, "I am fine. I am free." Take a fourth step and say, "I am moving on." You can say these affirmations aloud when you're alone, but say them mentally when others are present.

Do this every time that you pass over the buried paper. You will need this little ritual for a while, but in time you will begin to forget it. That is when your true healing begins, when you stop needing the ritual. There will later come a time when you can no longer remember exactly where you buried the paper, or perhaps even why you buried it. Finally the whole thing will seem absurd to you, and that is when you'll be sure that the spell has fully manifested.

⚜ One Big Thing Spell ⚜

Are you basically okay, except for one big thing that you just can't seem to forget or move beyond? Whether it is an injustice, a victimization, a loss, a failure, an illness, a missed opportunity, a disaster, a mistake, a historic event, a person you can't seem to get over, or something else, this spell can help you to finally get past it. It is an outdoor spell that is best cast on a bright day in pleasant weather. You will need:

+ a white balloon with a string attached to it (A helium-filled balloon is best, but one blown up by mouth will do.)
+ a felt-tip pen
+ four sticks of incense (Use four sticks of the same scent. Make this cedar, copal, dragon's blood, frankincense, myrrh, patchouli, or sandalwood, if possible.)

Preparation

Give deep thought to the problem or issue you need to get over. Reduce it to a few words, and write them on the balloon. Blow it up, and tie the string to it. You are going to release it as part of the spell, so if you are concerned about someone seeing you or finding your balloon, turn it inside out and write on it, then turn it right side out and blow it up.

Select a location to cast the spell. This should be an open place that has no tree branches or power lines overhead. It should also be a somewhat private site where you are not likely to be interrupted. A helium balloon will soar without wind, but you should wait for a breezy day to cast the spell if you use an air-filled one.

The Spell

Take the balloon and the incense to the place you have chosen. Secure the balloon. Get into a magickal mood, raise power, and light the sticks of incense. Face each of the cardinal points in turn as you cast the spell. Begin by turning to the North and saying:

> *Guardians of the North,*
> *Powers of Earth, powers of clarity,*
> *Make this spell a reality.*

Push one stick of incense into the ground. Turn to the East and say:

> *Guardians of the East,*
> *Powers of Air, powers of thought,*
> *Make this spell work as sought.*

Push another stick of incense into the ground. Turn to the South and say:

> *Guardians of the South,*
> *Powers of Fire, powers of energy,*
> *Make this spell work immediately.*

Push a stick of incense into the ground. Turn to the West and say:

Guardians of the West,
Powers of Water, powers of emotion,
Put this spell into motion.

Push the last stick of incense into the ground, and grasp the balloon by its string.

Stand in the center of the space that you have defined with the incense sticks, holding the balloon. Concentrate on releasing your issue with the balloon. Hold it up, and let go of the string. Watch the balloon take flight, and visualize the burden that you have been carrying soaring away from you. You should feel uplifted and relieved as the balloon moves away from you. It's fine if it pops while you're watching it.

Remain there until the incense burns down. Ground the power that you raised, and clean up.

Afterward

Whenever something reminds you of your one big thing, recall the sight of that balloon soaring away from you. Remember that this thing no longer has anything to do with you, and rejoice in your freedom from it.

∴ Personal Power Talisman ∾

Your personal power is based on your strengths, abilities, and potential. A Personal Power Talisman is a tool that can help you to overcome doubts, build self-confidence, succeed with spells, live a magickal life, and achieve your full potential. Its magick begins as soon as you begin to think about making it. The talisman is most powerful when made slowly, over time, with deep thought, great care, and exquisite attention to detail.

The spell for the final enchantment of the completed talisman is best cast at midnight on the night of a Full Moon (use a calendar to time it). You can make these talismans for other people, but they are best made personally by the one who wishes to fully activate his or her powers.

Some of the many ways to use this talisman include handling it before performing divination, such as casting the I Ching or reading tarot cards; placing it on your altar while you cast spells; keeping it at hand while you study or take tests; putting it under your pillow to augment your dream work; and touching it whenever you need a magickal boost. To make a Personal Power Talisman you will need:

+ a piece of cloth in your favorite color and texture

+ needle and thread to sew a mojo bag

+ a piece of gold cord or ribbon that is long enough to tie eight knots in

+ eight personal power charms (See the list below.)

+ cinnamon powder, essential oil, or a cinnamon stick

+ a pentacle or pentagram (Any type will do, even the symbol ⊛ drawn on a piece of paper.)

+ your favorite incense

+ a candle in your favorite scent and color

+ paint, markers, beads, or embroidery thread with which to decorate the mojo bag

Preparation

Use the cloth and the cord to fashion a mojo bag that is small enough to easily fit into a pocket, handbag, briefcase, or backpack. Draw, embroider, or otherwise decorate the bag with a personal power symbol such as your power animal, your totem animal, or the symbol for your astrological sign (see below). This is your talisman, so you should make it in whatever way looks good and feels right to you.

The Spell

Fill the bag with eight small personal power charms. These should be things that resonate with power for you. For example, if you have a power animal or a totem animal, you could include a picture or other small image of it. If you have a "lucky" stone or coin that has been with you for years, you might wish to include that, and so on. Use whatever charms you like, but it is best to use natural things that have been acquired without causing harm, such as feathers that birds have shed, rather than feathers that were plucked from their bodies. Leaves or branches that have fallen from trees are preferable to those torn from living trees. Use seeds or flowers that have been gathered without leaving a plant unable to reproduce itself, and so on.

Charms that are purchased, such as spices, are just as effective as those that have been wildcrafted. Herbs and other plants are best used dried, rather than fresh, to prevent spoilage in the mojo bag. Images of animals might include pictures, small statues, carvings, and the like. If you work in a zoo and have access to the shed fur of a lion or live on a farm and have access to goat hair or horsehair, those are more powerful charms than images.

Astrology can be used to select personal power charms. If you know your Moon sign and your rising sign as well as your Sun sign, you may want to include charms to represent them too. Here is a list of signs and the charms you might include for each.

♈ **Aries**: A talisman for an Aries is best begun on a Tuesday, their personal power day. Appropriate ingredients for it include alder bark or leaves, allspice berries, basil, bloodstones, red carnation petals, cayenne pepper, cedar (chips, tips, or shavings), cloves, crystals, cumin seeds, dandelion (roots, leaves, or flowers), red feathers, fennel seeds, garlic capsules, red geranium petals, candied ginger, chili peppers, gold coins or charms, iron rings, juniper berries, marjoram, mustard seeds, onion flakes, peppercorns, pinecones or pineneedles, images of rams, rosemary, red stones, thyme, and red wool.

♉ **Taurus:** A talisman for a Taurus is best begun on a Friday, their personal power day. Appropriate ingredients for it include dried apple slices, dried apricots, small brass bells, images of bulls or cows, cardamom pods, carnation petals, cedar (tips, chips, or shavings), cherry pits, clover, copper coins or charms, daisy petals, dandelion (root, leaves, or flowers), hawthorn flowers, heather, hibiscus, jasmine, lilac, lily of the valley, magnolia leaves or flowers, images of minotaurs, oakmoss, orchids, raspberry leaves, rose hips, saffron threads, sage, green or blue stones, dried strawberries, thyme, images of white tigers, vanilla beans, violet leaves or flowers, wicker pieces, and willow bark or leaves.

♊ **Gemini:** A talisman for a Gemini is best begun on a Wednesday, their personal power day. Appropriate ingredients for it include two almonds, aniseed, two caraway seeds, two pieces of citron peel, clover, two crystals, two images of deer, two dill seeds, two fennel seeds, gladiola petals, hawthorn (bark, blossoms, or leaves), two horehound candies, two iris flowers, lavender, lily petals, lemongrass, mace, marjoram, orris root (whole or powdered), parsley, two pear seeds, two peppermint candies, yellow rose petals, snapdragon blossoms, images of twins, lemon verbena, and two bicolored, iridescent, or multicolored stones.

♋ **Cancer:** A talisman for a Cancerian is best begun on a Monday, their personal power day. Appropriate ingredients for it include small aloe spears, amber, beach glass, catnip, chamomile, images of crabs, daisy petals, driftwood, eucalyptus leaves, gardenia, white geranium

petals, silver glitter, honeysuckle, jasmine, larkspur
petals, lemon balm, lemon peel, lotus nut, marigold,
mimosa (bark, leaves, or flowers), moonstones,
moonwort (also called honesty), pansies, poppy seeds,
pastel stones, white rose petals, rose quartz, sand,
scarabs, sea shells, images of the Moon, silver coins or
rings, lemon verbena, and violet leaves or flowers.

♌ **Leo**: A talisman for a Leo is best begun on a Sunday,
their personal power day. Appropriate ingredients
for it include acorns, angelica, aniseed, bay leaves,
chamomile, chicory, cloves, dill seeds, gold coins or
rings, gold glitter, goldenseal, hazel nuts, juniper (bark,
leaves, or berries), images of lions, marigold, nutmegs,
oak leaves, orange peels, peony petals, rosemary, saffron
threads, sunstones (sparkling feldspar), images of
sphinxes, images of the Sun, yellow or golden stones,
sunflower seeds or petals, and tiger's-eyes.

♍ **Virgo**: A talisman for a Virgo is best begun on a
Wednesday, their personal power day. Appropriate
ingredients for it include almonds, amethysts, aster
petals, images of brown bears, caraway seeds, citron
peels, cornflowers, cypress bark or leaves, dill leaves
or seeds, fennel seeds, grape leaves or vine tendrils,
hazelnuts, horehound candies, lily petals, mace,
marjoram, morning glory vines or flowers, moss,
narcissus bulb or petals, nickels, peppermint, raisins,
rosemary, savory, violet leaves or flowers, and gray,
brown, or tan stones.

♎ **Libra**: A talisman for a Libra is best begun on a Friday,
their personal power day. Appropriate ingredients for it
include small aloe spears, dried apple slices, catnip,
copper coins or charms, black feathers, royal blue glitter,

lilac blossoms, magnolia leaves or flowers, marigold petals, marjoram, orchids, rose petals, pennyroyal, spearmint candies, blue stones, sugar cubes, toy swords, thyme, vanilla beans, vanilla sugar, lemon verbena, and violet leaves or flowers.

♏ **Scorpio**: A talisman for a Scorpio is best begun on a Tuesday, their personal power day. Appropriate ingredients for it include allspice berries, anemone petals, ash bark or leaves, basil, red chrysanthemum petals, cloves, copper coins or charms, cumin seeds, cypress bark or leaves, dill seeds, small geodes, iron rings, ivy leaves, nettles, obsidian, pine cones or needles, pomegranate seeds, saffron threads, images of scorpions, steel bands or rings, dark red stones, thistles, yucca leaves, and eagle, vulture, or hawk feathers.

♐ **Sagittarius**: A talisman for a Sagittarius is best begun on a Thursday, their personal power day. Appropriate ingredients for it include acorns, amethysts, aniseed, aster petals, arrowheads, toy bows and arrows, purplish carnation petals, images of centaurs, cedar (tips, chips, or shavings), patterned cloth, red clover, daffodil petals, dried figs, candied ginger, holly leaves or berries, images of horses, juniper (bark, leaves, or berries), myrtle leaves or blossoms, nutmegs, rosemary, sage, spruce cones or needles, star anise, purplish stones, tinfoil or tin charms, and turquoise.

♑ **Capricorn**: A talisman for a Capricorn is best begun on a Wednesday, their personal power day. Appropriate ingredients for it include birch bark or leaves, pieces of coal, dark red or russet carnation petals, chervil, crystals, cypress (bark, buds, or leaves), flax seed oil capsules, holly leaves or berries, horny goatweed, lead, images of goats, goose down or feathers, holly leaves or berries, magnolia leaves or flowers, mint, oakmoss, poppy seeds, rue, sassafras, slippery elm, sorrel, black stones, thyme, and zircons.

♒ **Aquarius**: A talisman for an Aquarian is best begun on a Saturday, their personal power day. Appropriate ingredients for it include almonds, aluminum foil or charms, amber, amethysts, aniseed, ash leaves or bark, aspen leaves, bittersweet berries, buttercup flowers, citron peels, white coral, clear quartz crystals, cypress leaves or bark, daffodil petals, dandelion (root, leaves, or flowers), fennel seeds, flax seed oil capsules, lavender, lead, mace, images of otters, peppermint, pine cones or needles, poppy seeds, rosemary, sage, snowdrop blossoms, images of stars, silver coins or charms, lemon verbena, and violet leaves or flowers.

♓ **Pisces**: A talisman for a Pisces is best begun on a Wednesday, their personal power day. Appropriate ingredients for it include alder bark or leaves, amethysts, aniseed, ash bark or leaves, blue, white, or green carnation petals, catnip, cloves, coral, pale blue or sea-green cotton thread or cotton cloth, eucalyptus leaves, fish oil capsules, images of fish, gardenias, blue hyacinth florets, lemon peel, lilac blossoms, mother-of-pearl, Norfolk Island pine needles, nutmegs, rue, sage, star anise, tinfoil or tin charms, and willow bark or leaves.

After filling the bag, add the cinnamon, and tie the mojo bag shut with eight knots. If you are using essential oil of cinnamon, anoint the bag with it after you tie the knots. Place the completed talisman on a pentacle, and position it to charge in moonlight for one or more nights.

The Spell

Choose an appropriate day, such as your personal power day, or a day when the Sun or Moon is in your astrological sign (an astrological almanac will have that information). Midnight is the best time for the working.

When you are ready to cast the spell, collect the incense, candle, pentacle, and mojo bag. Get into a magickal mood, and create sacred space around the area where you will be working.

Place the pentacle on your altar or other working surface, and place everything else atop it in a manner that is pleasing to you. Light the candle, then light the incense from the candle. Raise power. Use your projective hand to hold the talisman in the incense smoke, turning it so that the entire mojo bag will be smudged. As you do this, say:

By moonlight and midnight,
By starlight and insight,
By smoke and candlelight,
I accept my birthright.

Beginning with North and working deosil, face each direction in turn as you hold the talisman up and say:

Charged on this day, and at this hour,
To help me grow and let me flower,
By the powers of the Lord of each Watchtower,
This talisman will stimulate my personal power.
By the powers of the Lord of each Watchtower,
This talisman will activate my personal power!

Place the talisman back on the pentacle when you finish, and leave it there until the candle and the incense have burned out. Monitor them until they finish burning. Concentrate on pouring all the power of the spell into the talisman. Envision the way you expect the talisman to work for you. When the candle guts out, ground the power that you raised and clean up.

Afterward

The more that you use it, touch it, and think about it, the more powerful this talisman will become. Keep it with you whenever possible. To renew its magick, place it in moonlight overnight, or smudge it with incense.

When you feel that you no longer need your talisman, it can then be buried, burned, thrown out, put away in a safe place, or disposed of in whatever way seems best to you. Charms such as stones may be cleared (see "stones" under "Spell Ingredients" on page xviii) and retained for future use, if you like.

~2~

Goals, Hopes, Wishes

To set a goal, have a hope, or make a wish is to place a marker on the road map of your life. How do you get there from here? Spells in this chapter can help you with that.

~ Countdown Spell ~

Do you have a goal that seems difficult to reach? Would you like to change yourself or improve your life in some way? Whatever your personal goal may be, if it's reasonable and feasible, this simple but powerfully effective spell can help you to achieve it.

Casting a spell is not enough to reach most goals, of course. You must also make practical efforts, such as working out, saving money, attending classes, or whatever your goal requires.

For this spell you will need:

+ paper
+ a writing implement (Use a freshly sharpened pencil if you wish to erase your goal to keep it confidential.)
+ a stick of incense
+ *Optional*: If you happen to own a sapphire, garnet, or turquoise ring, wear it on your projective hand while you cast the spell or work it afterward.

Preparation

Clearly and specifically identify your goal. This is a crucial part of the spell, so give it careful consideration. Meditation helps with this.

Next, consider paths to your goal, and formulate at least one action plan. Set a realistic time period for reaching the goal. This might be one month, one year, five years, or another length of time, depending on the nature of your goal.

The Spell

Once your goal is clear in your mind, get into a magickal mood. Gather the spell materials, and place them on the altar or other working surface. Raise power, and create sacred space around your working area. Light the incense.

Concentrate on your goal, and visualize it as already achieved. For example, if your goal is to finish school, you could envision yourself waving your diploma in the air at the graduation ceremony; if your goal is to buy a house, you could see its key in your hand as you unlock the door on moving day. Once your visualization is complete, take a mental snapshot of it, and keep your focus on that as you proceed.

Hold the writing implement in the incense smoke, and concentrate on charging its ink or lead with magick. Do this until the incense burns itself out, then ground power and clean up. Leave the writing implement in moonlight overnight, perhaps on a windowsill.

The next day, use the pen or pencil to write your goal at the top of the paper. If you are using a pencil because your goal is confidential, write it down and then erase it. No one will be able to read your goal, but the paper will still be imprinted with it.

Count the days that you have allotted for reaching your goal, and write this number beneath it. If your time frame for the spell is lengthy, you may need to tape several sheets of paper together. Hang the paper in a place where you will see it every day, such as on a closet door.

Begin the countdown. Each morning, from then until the goal is achieved, use the charged writing implement to cross off the number at the top of the page and write the next lower number beneath it. For example, if you have allowed one year to reach your goal, you will be writing 365, 364, 363, 362, and so on, as the days pass. Say this affirmation (or an affirmation of your own devising) aloud each morning when you cross off a number and write a new one:

> *I am strong. I am determined.*
> *Nothing will distract me, divert me,*
> *or prevent me from reaching my goal.*

Afterward

Continue the countdown. Take at least one small step toward your goal every day, and you are likely to achieve it before the countdown is finished.

⁓ Footsteps Spell ⁓

What are your career goals? Whose footsteps would you like to follow in? Do you hope to succeed in a career that is difficult to gain entrée to?

Some careers can be hard to launch for a variety of reasons. Industries that are considered glamorous, such as fashion, broadcasting, and entertainment, can be hard to break into because there are so many applicants for every job opening. Other careers, such as spaceflight, ballet, or surgery, require many years of very specialized training. Still other careers, such as those in politics, can be hard to enter without support or financial backing from others. The challenges to getting started in such professions can be daunting.

If you have the talent or ability to make it in a certain career but just can't seem to get your foot in the door, this spell can help you. It will not make you a success at something you are unsuited to, or unqualified for, but it will help you to find employment in the industry of your choice.

Footprints have been considered magickal in many cultures since ancient times. Footprint magick is traditionally worked by physically lifting the dirt in which someone has stepped. Surfaces are mostly paved in our times, but we can still work footprint magick by adapting it to present circumstances. For this spell you will need:

+ several strips of wide adhesive tape, such as masking tape or duct tape

+ a pentacle or pentagram (Any type will do, even the symbol ⊛ drawn on a piece of paper.)

+ an orange candle

+ a stick of incense

+ a box, pouch, bottle, or other container in which to keep the spell materials

+ *Optional*: pink carnation petals

Preparation

Collect footprints from people who are already doing the kind of work that you hope to do one day. To accomplish this, identify a place where people are engaged in this type of work. It might be a firehouse, if you hope to be a firefighter; a hospital, if you hope to be a doctor or nurse; a theater, if you hope to be an actor or set designer; a brokerage house or stock exchange if you hope to be a trader or stockbroker; and so on.

Next, identify the best location for gathering their footprints. If you hope to be a stage actor, for example, it would be better to collect footprints from the area just outside the stage door than from the sidewalk in front of the theater; if you hope to be a judge, it would be better to collect footprints outside a judges' entrance or elevator than from the courthouse steps; and so on.

Go to this location, preferably at a time when you are not likely to be observed or interrupted. Stick a strip of tape to the ground, then rip it up. Hold the strip to the wind (or blow on it, if the air is still). Visualize any extraneous footprints—such as those of delivery people or passersby—being blown away and erased from the tape. When you feel that only the footprints you seek are on the tape, roll it up (sticky side inward) so that it forms a tight tube or cylinder. Repeat this process with several more strips of tape.

Take the cylinders of tape home, and place them in the center of a pentacle until you are ready to cast the spell. If you are using carnations, work deosil to sprinkle the petals around the circle of the pentacle. It isn't a problem if these dry out before the spell is cast.

The Spell

Gather all the spell ingredients. Get into a magickal mood, and create sacred space around the area where you will be working. Place the candle on the pentacle with the tape cylinders, and raise power. Light the candle, then light the incense from it.

Focus on the result you want the spell to have. Visualize yourself working happily in your chosen career. Raise your arms and say:

> *By Minerva and Apollo,*
> *In their footsteps I will follow.*
> *As I will, so mote it be.*
> *I will work in this industry!*

Hold each roll of tape in the incense smoke for a few moments, while concentrating on charging it with the magick of your intent. Drip a little wax on each cylinder to seal the spell. Focus on the brilliant career that you envision for yourself, and monitor the candle and incense until they burn themselves out.

Place the cylinders of tape in the container, along with the ashes from the incense (and the carnation petals, if you have used them). Drip some wax over the container's opening to further seal the spell, then ground the power that you raised.

Afterward

Keep the container of spell ingredients in a safe place until the spell has fully manifested. Take it out and handle it or keep it near you whenever you are working toward your goal, by taking courses or applying for jobs, for example. You can discard the container once you have become established in your career.

⌁ Interview Charm ⌁

It usually takes several interviews to land a job, so prepare several of these charms when you're looking for work. To make them you will need:

+ several strips of wide adhesive tape, such as masking tape or duct tape
+ a pair of shoes that you are likely to wear to interviews or for work

The Spell

Take tape impressions of your own footsteps, or of the bottoms of your shoes. Roll them up tightly into cylinders. Carry one with you whenever you go on an audition or job interview. If you decide that you would like to have the position you applied for, leave the charm behind when you go. This will help you to "get your foot in the door." Leave the charm in a place where it is not likely to be noticed for a long time, such as in a planter.

⸱ Star of Ḣope Spell ⸱

Do you have a secret hope? Something that you have never told anyone? That hope is not likely to ever be realized unless you do something about it. One magickal action that you can take is to communicate your secret hope to the Universe. This spell will do that, so do not cast it (or even think about casting it) unless you are absolutely certain that you want your hope to be realized. You should feel hopeful while you cast this spell, so don't attempt it if you are feeling sad, negative, angry, or pessimistic. It can be cast at any time, but it is best begun on the night of a New Moon (use a calendar to time it), and completed on the night of the next Full Moon. The spell is most powerful if the Sun or the Moon is in Aquarius on either night (an astrological almanac will have that information). You will need:

+ the Star card from a tarot deck (One from any tarot deck will do, but if you have a choice, use a card that depicts a woman pouring water from a jar.)

+ a tin box (No substitutions, it must be tin. The container can be any shape, but it should have a cover and be large enough to hold the tarot card. The tins in which biscuits and crackers are sometimes packaged are good for this purpose. You can use the box as it is, or you can paint it, line it, or decorate it, if you feel this will enhance your spell.)

+ a white feather

+ a piece of paper (Any sort of paper will do, but it's nice to use high-quality paper.)

+ a pencil with an eraser

+ two sticks of incense (Any kind is fine, but use violet if you happen to have it.)

+ a pentacle or pentagram (Any type will do, even the symbol ⊕ drawn on a piece of paper.)

+ *Optional*: If you happen to own an opal ring, wear it on your projective hand while you cast the spell.

Preparation

Get into a magickal mood. Assemble all of the spell ingredients, and create sacred space for the working. Place the pentacle on your altar or other working surface, with its top point facing East. Center the box on the pentacle.

The Spell

Light one stick of incense, and raise power. Put the tarot card in the middle of the box, then close it. Open your hands and hold them over the box, with your palms facing downward. Focus on your hope, and say:

> *Goddess Pandora, Giver of All Gifts,*
> *I thank you for giving us*
> *The powerful gift of hope.*
> *I name this box Pandora's Box.*
> *If it will do no harm,*
> *I ask you to fulfill the hope*
> *That you will find within it.*

Use the pencil to write your secret hope on the paper. Be totally honest and very specific about what you hope for. Erase what you have written. Your hope will still be a secret, but the paper will contain it nonetheless. Open the box, and put the paper in it under the tarot card. If you must fold the paper in order to make it fit, fold it three times. Place the feather on top of the card, then close the box.

Ground the power that you raised, and clean up. Keep the box atop the pentacle, and put them in a safe place, such as beneath your bed or on your altar. Leave them there for two weeks—or until the Full Moon, if you began the spell on the New Moon.

Do not open the box until you are ready to complete the spell. If possible, keep the top point of the pentacle oriented toward the East. Concentrate on your hope during this period, focusing on the exact form that you want its fulfillment to take.

When you are ready to complete the spell, put the box, pentacle, and the second stick of incense on your altar or other working surface. Orient the top point of the pentacle toward the East, and remove the feather from the box. Close it, and place the incense atop the box. Get into a magickal mood. Light the incense, and raise power. Use the feather to fan the smoke upward as you say:

> *Goddess Pandora, Giver of All Gifts,*
> *Anesidora, She Who Sends Up Gifts,*
> *Receive my hope!*

Repeat this phrase as many times as seems necessary to you while the incense burns. Visualize your hope ascending to a place where the entire Universe will sense its reverberation. When the incense is half spent, begin talking to Pandora. Speak to her sincerely, in your natural voice, as you would to a friend whom you are asking for an important favor. Explain why you hold this hope and what outcome you would like to have when the hope is fulfilled.

This is a very important part of the spell, because omitting it can cause the spell to go wrong. Suppose your secret hope is to get a certain job. Without specifying the outcome, you might get the job because you cast this spell, but find that the job makes you so miserable that you wind up leaving it.

Talk to Pandora until the incense has finished burning. Thank her for listening, then end the spell. Ground the power that you raised, and put the tarot card back in its deck. Bury the paper, because Pandora is an Earth goddess. You can reuse the box and keep the feather as a charm if you like, or bury them with the paper.

Wish Spells

The old adage is true: be careful what you wish for. The danger with wishes isn't that they won't come true; it's that they will come true, but not in the way that was meant, or with the results that were intended. Consider all possible outcomes before making a wish. Be realistic, word it precisely, and proceed with caution.

If you happen to own a piece of emerald or carnelian jewelry, wear it while casting your wish spell.

⁓ Lords of Air Spell ⁓

When we say that something is "in the air" or "blowing in the wind," we mean that it is available or likely to happen. One of the many ways to make a wish is to literally put the wish into the wind.

Nearly every human culture has had gods who rule the element of Air. Examples include wind gods such as Aeolus (Greek), Skan (Native American), Aquilo (Roman), Feng Po (Chinese), Stribog (Slavic), and Njord (Norse). This spell, which invokes all the Lords of Air to grant your wish, is best cast on a windy night. You will need:

+ a piece of white or pale blue paper with your wish written on it (If you like, you can use a color of ink that relates to your wish, such as pink or red for love, green for money, orange for success, black for banishing, and so on.)

+ your favorite perfume, cologne, or aftershave

+ a flat, shallow container, such as a tray or dish

+ a stick of incense (Ginseng, sage, lavender, sandalwood, and violet are good choices, if you happen to have one of them on hand.)

+ *Optional*: finely chopped, powdered, or crumbled herbs that relate to your wish (See the list below.)

Preparation

Assemble the spell ingredients. Light the incense, get into a magickal mood, and create sacred space around the area where you will be working. Take the paper on which you have written your wish, and spray or anoint it with the perfume. Don't be concerned if this causes the ink to run or smear, because the paper will still hold your wish. Focus on your wish, with particular concentration on the end result that you would like it to have. Waft the paper through the air a few times to dry the perfume, then pass it repeatedly through the incense smoke. The paper should then be scented.

Focus on your wish again, as you cut or tear the paper into confetti-sized pieces. Sprinkle these onto the tray.

Optional: If you are using herbs, sprinkle a large spoonful of them into the tray and mix them with the pieces of paper. Here are examples of some of the commonplace herbs that correspond to different types of wishes:

Ambition, Goals:	bay leaves
Attraction:	cinnamon
Clarity:	dandelion, lemongrass
Confidence:	cardamom, turmeric
Fertility:	pine, flour
Fidelity:	chili powder
Friendship:	lemon zest, lavender
Happiness:	catnip, marigold
Increase:	rosemary
Health:	garlic, thyme
Job, Career:	pecan
Justice:	cedar
Love, Romance:	rose, carnation
Money, Finances:	mint, clover
Reversal:	sage
Success:	ginger, basil

Herbs can be used singly or combined. For example, if you wish to get a raise at work, you might use mint, rosemary, and ground pecans. If you wish to get pregnant, you might add flour and ginger to the tray, but if you wish for justice, you might use ginger and finely ground cedar chips. If you wish to find a mate, you might add cinnamon and carnation petals. If you wish to get out of debt, you might use sage, and so on.

The Spell

Get into a magickal mood, and take the container outside at night. Raise power. Hold it up, face East, and say:

> Gods of Winds, Lords of Air,
> Grant my wish if it be fair.

Place the tray in a place where the wind is likely to reach it, such as on a lawn chair or balcony railing. Concentrate on your wish, and say again:

> Gods of Winds, Lords of Air,
> Grant my wish if it be fair.

Visualize your wish going forth into the world with the wind, and becoming manifest. Ground the power that you raised.

Leave the container outdoors all night, and check on it the next morning. It is a positive sign if you find the container empty, but a negative omen if anything remains in it.

∴ Lady of the Lake Spell ∾

Every lake is presided over by a goddess or female nature spirit. It isn't necessary to know her name in order to call upon her powers, because you can address her by the title of Lady of the Lake.

This spell can be cast early on any day (except when the lake is frozen), but it is best cast at dawn on a misty morning. You will need:

+ a small glass bottle with a cork or cap

+ a red candle

+ a piece of paper with your wish written on it (If you like, you can use a color of ink that relates to your wish, such as pink for romance, dark blue for justice, light blue for peace, orange for action, red for strength, purple for wisdom, green for healing or fertility, and so on.)

+ enough sunflower seeds to fill the bottle (Substitute sunflower oil or sunflower petals if the neck of your bottle is too narrow for sunflower seeds to pass through it. Don't be concerned if you use oil and the ink runs, because your words will still be in the bottle.)

Preparation

Get into a magickal mood, and gather the spell ingredients. Light the candle, and create sacred space around the area where you will be working. Keep repeating your wish aloud as you prepare the spell bottle.

Roll up the paper on which you have written your wish, and insert it into the bottle. Fill the bottle with the sunflower seeds, and seal it. Drip candle wax over the top of the bottle to create a waterproof seal. Use as much wax as you like for this, until the bottle looks magickal and feels enchanted to you.

Place the bottle beside the candle. Concentrate on your wish, as you monitor the candle until it burns itself out. The spell bottle is then ready.

The Spell

Take the bottle to a lake. The spell will be cast when the bottle is thrown into the water, so choose a good spot from which to do this.

Breathe deeply. Listen to the sounds of the lake and any of its creatures who may be up and about. Notice the colors,

scents, and beauty of the location. Allow yourself to experience the magick of the lake. Raise power, and say aloud:

> *Awake, awake, Lady of this Lake!*
> *I will give my wish for you to take.*
> *By the power of daybreak,*
> *Please grant it quickly, for my sake.*

Shake the spell bottle, and say:

> *Lady of the Lake, awaken!*
> *Bottle shaken, bottle taken,*
> *Don't grant my wish if I'm mistaken.*
> *Lady of this Lake, awaken!*
> *Bottle shaken, bottle taken,*
> *Heart's wish unforsaken,*
> *No harm done when it's betaken!*

Throw the bottle into the lake, as far out as you can, as you say
again:

> *Awake, awake, Lady of this Lake!*
> *I give my wish for you to take.*
> *By the power of daybreak,*
> *Please grant it quickly, for my sake.*

Ground the power that you raised. Contemplate the lake quietly for a few minutes, then leave.

Afterward

Remember to thank the Lady of the Lake when your wish is
granted. If your wish is not granted, know that this is because
granting it would have caused harm to you, or to someone else.
Meditate on your wish. Look for any ethical problems with it.
Try to think of another way of making the wish (such as wishing for the love of a good person, rather than the love of a specific person; or wishing for a better job, rather than wishing

for someone else's job). If you can come up with an alternate wish, ask the Lady of the Lake to grant that.

◌ Ocean Mother Spell ◌

Yemaya, the Ocean Mother, is a benevolent goddess who helps human beings in many ways. Originally an African river goddess, her worship was brought to the New World by Africans who had been kidnapped into slavery. It spread through North America, South America, and the Caribbean. She became known by different names in different lands, but by whatever name she is called, Yemaya is known for her willingness to respond to human calls for help.

This spell should be cast at a beach on a moonlit night, while the tide is coming in. It is most powerfully cast beneath a Full Moon or a Crescent Moon (use a calendar to time this). You will need:

- ✦ seven blue, white, or silver candles
- ✦ a stick of sandalwood incense
- ✦ a piece of beautiful blue, white, or silver cloth
- ✦ a piece of blue, white, or silver ribbon
- ✦ a piece of blue or white paper with your wish written on it, preferably in silver ink
- ✦ fish food (Get this from a pet supplies shop.)
- ✦ seven small offerings (Appropriate offerings to Yemaya include fans, flowers, jewelry, sea shells, crystals, coral, soap, perfume, grain, and yams. Use small items such as tiny shells, pieces of yam, miniature bottles of perfume, and so on, for this spell.)

Preparation

This spell begins when you first consider which offerings to use. It grows in power as you gather the offerings and make

the offering bundle. The spell is cast when you offer the bundle
to Yemaya. You do that by leaving it where the sea will take it,
so it is helpful to study the tidal patterns at your beach for several days before you cast the spell. Choose an offering site that
the tide is sure to reach. If you will need to toss the offering
off a jetty or down onto rocks, that's fine.

Assemble all the spell ingredients, except the candles and
incense. Get into a magickal mood, and create sacred space
around the area where you will be working. Lay the cloth flat
upon your altar or other working surface. Put the paper with
your wish in the center of the cloth, and place your seven offerings on top of that. Sprinkle the fish food over the offerings.
Wrap the cloth around everything to create a small bundle.
Wrap the bundle tightly with the ribbon, and tie it with seven
knots. You should have a small, attractively wrapped package
when you finish.

The Spell

Go to the beach at the appointed time. Arrange the candles on
the sand in any way that pleases you, then light them. Get into
a magickal mood, and raise power. Light the incense from one
of the candles, and stick it into the sand. Pass your offering
through the incense smoke seven times, then place it reverently in your offertory site. Say:

> Ocean Mother, Queen of the Sea,
> Hear my plea and answer me.
> Mother of Secrets, Mother of Fish,
> Accept my gift, and grant my wish.
> By the power of moonlight,
> Grant my wish if it be right.

Monitor the candles until they burn themselves out, then
ground the power that you raised. It is best if you can remain
on the beach until the tide comes all the way in, and then goes
out. It is a good omen if the waves immediately snatch your

offering and drag it out to sea. If the sea does not accept your offering, or if it is returned with an incoming tide, your wish is not likely to be granted.

~·3·~

Love

What brings you to needing a love spell? Is there an empty place in your heart, your bed, or your life? Would you like companionship? Do you yearn for love? Do you need a lover?

Magick can definitely help with these things, but love spells are tricky. You have to be careful with them. To cast a selfish or mean-spirited "love spell" is a magickal mistake. Even if the spell seems to work, it will ultimately backfire on you in some way.

The love spells in this chapter are meant for single people who are free to enter new relationships with other single people. These are spells that you cast for yourself, not for others. They invite love rather than compelling it. If you use them as directed, there will be no magickal backlash from them.

~· Goddess of Love Spell ·~

When you need love, you can turn to the Love Goddess for help. Venus, Atargatis, Aphrodite, Ishhara . . . the Goddess of Love has been known by different names in various cultures throughout human history. This spell invokes her by many of those names, to alert her that you are available to give and receive love. Recognize that love works best when it is mutual, reciprocal. You will have the most success with this spell if you focus on what you want to give, as well as on what you hope to get, while you cast it.

The spell takes five days to complete. It is best begun five days before the Full Moon (use a calendar to time it). If you seek passionate love, cast it at night rather than during the day. You will need:

+ five sticks of floral incense

+ a large pink candle

+ a tray

+ as many of the following things as you can obtain: green and pink stones, green and pink glitter, catnip, rosemary, pink flower petals, silver bells, hearts, a rose quartz, and anything that represents love to you

Preparation

Get into a magickal mood, and create sacred space around the area where you will be working. Place the tray on your altar or other working surface, and assemble the other spell ingredients on it in a manner that is pleasing to you.

As you do this, concentrate on the kind of love that you wish to invite into your life. Love takes many forms, so it is important to be specific in love spells. If you fail to make yourself clear, you might wind up with a new puppy instead of the lover you had in mind. Visualize what you want, and focus on it.

The Spell

Raise power. Light the candle, then light the incense from the candle. Concentrate on the love that you need. Don't focus on a specific person or on physical or character traits. Think about the way that the person your spell attracts will feel about you, on how that will make you feel, and on how you will make the other person feel. Paint a picture in your mind of how you would like things to be. Open your hands. Hold them slightly to your sides with the palms facing upward, and chant this incantation:

By Hera, by Rhea, by Olwen and Maia,
By Sarah, by Vara, by Oshun and Gaia,
By Goda, by Holda, by Allat and Inanna,
By Lada, by Milda, by Blathnat and Diana,
By Anahita, Esmerelda, Dictynna, and Ishhara,
By Cytherea, Syria Dea, Shekinah, and Ostara,
I declare myself ready to receive love!

Alter the final line of the spell to reflect the type of love that you seek. This might be "romantic love," "passionate love," "the true love of a good wo/man," or whatever is appropriate. Repeat the incantation three times, then extinguish the candle (preferably by wetting your fingers and pinching it out or by using a candle snuffer). Allow the incense to burn itself out, then ground the power that you raised.

Repeat the spell every day for five days. If candle wax or incense ashes get on the tray, consider them as adding to the magick and leave them there. Keep the tray in a place where you will often see it during the five days. Each time that you notice it, concentrate on the love that you wish to manifest in your life.

Disassemble the tray after you cast the final spell on the fifth day. Items that you wish to retain, such as the tray, should be washed in running water. Everything else should be buried near your home. If that isn't practical, bury the charms in a potted plant inside your home.

Afterward

Be mindful of the spell ingredients you buried, and remember that their magickal vibrations are working. Know in your bones that you have cast the spell effectively, and wait patiently but expectantly for the spell to manifest.

⌁ Alphabet Spell ⌁

What would your ideal mate be like? Would you like to find that person? This spell helps you to define your search and, if that person exists, to invite her or him into your life.

The spell can be cast at any time, but it is best completed at the hour of Venus (midnight on a Friday night). If you hope for someone who was born under a certain astrological sign, cast the spell when the Sun or Moon is in that sign (an astrological almanac or calendar will have this information).

Use caution, as always, when working with fire. You will need:

+ two sheets of nice paper
+ a pen with green ink
+ a fireproof container
+ a green candle
+ a vessel of water for fire safety
+ *Optional*: seven sprigs of parsley

Preparation

Write the letters of the alphabet down the left margin of one sheet of paper: A-I on the front and J-Z on the back. When that is done, begin writing down all the attributes and qualities that you would like your ideal mate to have. List them alphabetically. Here are some examples, to give you an idea of how to get started:

> A—*attractive, attentive, ardent, able, affectionate*
> F—*fit, fun, funny, faithful, financially secure*
> I—*interesting, independent, industrious, has integrity*
> S—*smart, sane, sober, single, serious, sexy, sophisticated*

Focus, give this deep consideration, and be thorough. Include in your list qualities such as physical attributes, character traits, personality, philosophy, politics, sexuality, and so on. Use positive terms instead of negative ones (e.g. "hardworking" or "career-oriented" rather than "not lazy"; "secure" instead of "not jealous"; "easygoing" rather than "not a control freak"; "generous" instead of "not cheap"; and so on). Include everything that you hope to receive from your mate, such as companionship, security, children, sexual satisfaction, or whatever is important to you. Don't forget to specify that the person should be single.

When you've finished, put the paper away in a safe place, and leave it there for a few days. Rework your list at least three times before you finalize the spell. Keep using the same sheet of paper. If you change your mind about something, cross it out. If you want to add something, do so. Each human being is unique. When you have finished, your paper may be nearly empty, or it may be almost illegible because so many things have been written on it. Whatever the case, it's fine. This is your spell, so you craft it in your own way.

The next step in the spell is to take the other sheet of paper and again write the alphabet down its margins. This time list all of your traits, quirks, attributes, and characteristics. Take your time. Be thorough, be brutally honest, and include positive things as well as negative ones. Omit nothing. Be sure to include everything that you hope to offer your mate, such as love, laughter, adventure, companionship, fidelity, children, great sex, a good life, a happy home, or whatever.

Place one sheet of paper on top of the other, and fold them together. Put the papers away, and leave them in a safe place for a few days.

The Spell

Put the fireproof container on your altar or other working surface, atop something that will not scorch if the bottom gets hot. Place the candle next to it. Put the water within reach. If you are using parsley, plait or entwine its sprigs into a rough wreath, and encircle the container with it.

Get into a magickal mood. Open a window, and create sacred space in the area where you will be working. Light the candle, and raise power. Review the lists one last time, and make any final changes that you like.

Take the page that you have made for your potential mate, turn it sideways, and scrawl across each side of it, "Send me what I need." Take the other page, turn it sideways, and scrawl on each side, "Send what is needed."

Place one page on top of the other, and refold them together several times. Concentrate on what you hope the spell will achieve, touch the papers to the candle flame, and drop them into the container. Keep focused on your goal while you watch them burn, and say:

> *So long as it will do no harm,*
> *Lead us to each other's arms.*
> *Love be deep, love be strong,*
> *Love be true, and last long.*

Make sure that the smoke from the burning paper is wafting out of the open window. You can use your hands to fan the smoke in that direction if need be. Be mindful of fire safety. Keep close watch on the container until the paper has been entirely consumed, then pour water into it. Monitor the candle until it burns itself out, then ground power and clean up.

Afterward

Assume an attitude of positive expectation until the spell manifests. Accept invitations, go to new places, and welcome opportunities to meet new people. Remember that the pickier you have been, the longer the spell may take to work.

⋰ Broadcast Spell ⋱

Love looks not with the eyes, but with the mind.
— Shakespeare, *A Midsummer Night's Dream*

If you hunger for love (or a lover) to enter your life, this spell is for you. It can be cast at any time, in any place where you have privacy and will not be interrupted, but it is best cast outdoors, from a balcony or other high place.

Optional: incense, music, candles, ritual garb, or whatever helps you to alter your consciousness

The Spell

Get into a magickal mood, and focus on your need. Lust and longing have different energy signatures, so be honest with yourself, and be clear about what you will be casting for. Raise power around that need. Concentrate on it, and form its raw emotion into a beam that you direct outward through your third eye. This is your call, which will draw someone to answer it. Say aloud:

I call from need, not from greed.
I call only that which will be good for me,
and do no harm to me or to others.

Mean it when you say this, because it is crucial to the ultimate success of the spell. The tricky part of this spell isn't getting someone to respond, it's getting the right person to answer.

Form your projective hand into a "megaphone," thus:

Hold it to your forehead over your third eye. Feel the power of your need and of the beam that directs your call. Envision the narrow beam radiating outward, like a sound wave, as it leaves your body. If it helps your visualization, picture the beam as

having a color or a sound. Amplify the power of the beam until it is strong enough to be sensed across your neighborhood, your town, or whatever calling area you have chosen.

Depending on where you are casting the spell, there will either be an arc of open space in front of you or a circle of open space around you. Slowly cover the entire open area with your beam, beginning and ending at the same point. Keep your hand to your third eye as you do this. If you hope that the person who answers your call will come from a particular direction, spend extra time focusing your beam there.

Sweep outward with your beam until you feel that your call has been fully transmitted. Ground the power that you raised, and leave that place. Eat something if you have trouble shaking off your magickal mood.

Afterward

This spell will manifest within ten days if your call has been strong enough. It will take longer or need to be repeated if you did not raise sufficient power.

Be open to new things while you are waiting for the spell to work. Break your habitual patterns. Do different things, and take advantage of opportunities to meet new people. If you have any preconceived notions about what the person who answers your call should look like, or be like, forget them. Be willing to be surprised, and wait expectantly.

If you have cast this spell twice, and two cycles of the Moon (two months) have passed without a response, it means that there is no one suitable in your calling area. Wait a few months and try the spell again, or go to a new location and cast it from there.

⸱ Come Back to Me Spell ⸱

Is there someone you would like to have back in your life? This spell is different from the others in the chapter because it does focus on a particular person. No matter what the cause of an estrangement, it isn't ethical to force someone's return. It is ethical, however, to ask the Universe to reunite you if you are meant to be together.

Whether it be a friend, lover, spouse, colleague, or family member, the best way to end an estrangement is usually non-magickal. Make an overture of some sort: apologize (or accept that person's apology), send a card, send flowers, invite the person out for coffee, have a heart-to-heart talk, and so on. But if there is some reason for avoiding these obvious methods, or if you have tried them without success, you could cast this spell. If you are nervous about how your attempt at reconciliation might be received, you could cast it as a prelude to making a nonmagickal overture.

In order for this spell to be ethical, you must be willing to accept the will of the gods (the Universe) as to whether or not you are to be reconciled. You must also be willing to accept whatever type of reconciliation is offered. For example, the door to a romantic relationship may be closed, but the door to a warm friendship could open instead. If you use this spell to try to impose your will upon someone else, it is more likely to backfire horribly upon you than it is to work in the way you desire.

The spell invokes Forseti, a Norse god whose dominion includes reconciliation as well as mediation and arbitration. He is said to always listen carefully to both sides in any disagreement, and he is noted for the fairness of his decisions. The spell can be cast at any time, but it is most powerful on the night of a Full Moon. You will need:

+ a pentacle or pentagram (Any type will do, even the symbol ✪ drawn on a piece of paper.)

+ a red candle

+ a carving tool

+ enough dried red or pink beans to outline the pentacle (These can be found in grocery stores.)

+ pictures and items that connect you with or remind you of the person you wish to be reconciled with (If you don't have any, write the person's name with red ink on pieces of paper and use them instead.)

+ *Optional*: a rose quartz

+ *Optional*: music that reminds you of this person

Preparation

Think about the person you want back. Concentrate on what you miss about him or her, and why you would like the two of you to be reconciled. Don't focus on what went wrong with your relationship, though, because you might be very much mistaken about what caused your estrangement. Instead, think about the benefits that a reunion would be likely to bring to each of you.

Identify and collect every object you possess that connects you and this person to each other. These might include such things as letters, photographs, gifts, books, souvenirs, items of clothing, e-mails, theater programs, and the like.

The Spell

Gather the spell ingredients. Carve the person's name or initials into the candle. If you are using music, turn it on (or begin to hum or sing it, if you prefer). Get into a magickal mood, and create sacred space around the area where you will be working.

Place the pentacle on your altar or other working surface, and put the candle in the center of the pentacle. Working deosil, place the beans around the circle of the pentacle. Arrange all the small items that connect the two of you around the pentacle; place any large items on or near the altar. If you are using a rose quartz, place it on the pentacle near the candle.

Raise power, and light the candle. Focus on the person and on healing the rift in your relationship. As the candle burns, open your arms wide and say,

As these words aloud are spoken,
Repair the ties that have been broken.
If it will harm none, and is meant to be,
Forseti, please bring _____ back to me.
If it be in accord with the Universe,
Restore _____ to me with this verse.
Forseti, He Who Stills All Strife,
Please return _____ to my life.
As these words aloud are spoken,
Heal the bond that has been broken.

Concentrate on welcoming this person back into your life, as you monitor the candle until it burns itself out. When it stops burning, ground the power that you raised. You should feel calm, and willing to accept whatever outcome the spell will have.

Clean up. Package all the personal items that you gathered for this spell. Put them away with the beans in a safe place for two full cycles of the Moon (two months), or until the spell has manifested. If you used a rose quartz, keep that with you as a charm during this period. Should two cycles of the Moon pass without any movement of this person back to you, it must be accepted that reconciliation does not seem to be the will of the gods at this time.

⋰4⋱

Life Enhancement

Magick is not a substitute for locking doors, consulting doctors, earning a living, or working on relationships. You can, however, enrich your life by using magick to attract the subtle energies that bring blessings such as abundance, prosperity, fertility, peace, and happiness.

⋰ Home Blessing Spell ⋱

Blessing your home helps to protect it and everyone who lives there. It attracts positive energy, such as friends and prosperity, and averts negative energy, such as unwanted visitors and negative entities and elementals. Blessing the home draws blessings to its inhabitants. We can all use all the blessings that we can get, so cast this spell as often as you like. Use it for a house, an apartment, or even a temporary home such as a dorm room. The spell invokes the Goddess in her triple aspect as Maiden, Mother, and Crone. That reflects the lunar phases of Waxing Moon, Full Moon, and Waning Moon, so this spell can be cast at any time. You will need:

- ✦ water (Spring water, rain water, or any other type of holy water is great, but ordinary tap water is fine.)
- ✦ salt (Sea salt is best, but ordinary table salt will do.)

+ a vessel, such as a chalice or bowl (You will be asperging your entire home with the water from this vessel, so choose one that will hold enough water for the operation.)

+ three sprigs of fresh herbs (Rosemary is best, sage is good, but use whatever herbs are available to you.)

+ blue or white ribbon (Substitute whatever you have on hand, if needed—even a rubber band will do.)

Preparation

Use the ribbon to tie the stems of the herbs together. Do this any way you like, but tie them securely and leave the leafy ends free.

The Spell

Get into a magickal mood. Assemble the spell ingredients, and create sacred space around the place where you will be working. Fill the vessel two-thirds full with water, and raise power.

Hold the vessel up with both hands. Regard the water, which will be vibrating slightly, and visualize it as a medium for the transference of magickal power. Do this in any way you like, such as by imagining the water suffused with light from within. Put the vessel down, and add a large pinch of salt to it. Use the bundle of herbs to stir the water deosil as you focus on your home and on drawing blessings to it. Think about the blessings you wish to attract. Visualize them reaching every member of the household, including pets.

When you feel that the water has been charged with your intent, carry it and the herb bundle to your front door. Hold the vessel in your receptive hand and the herbs in your projective hand. Dip the herbs in the water when you get to the door, and use them to draw a pentagram (⊛) on the back of the door. As you do this, say:

Goddess powerful, Goddess trine,
Grant blessings to this home of mine.

Dip the herbs in the water, and shake them to sprinkle a bit of water by the door, as you again say:

Goddess powerful, Goddess trine,
Grant blessings to this home of mine.

Proceed deosil through your entire home, carrying the vessel and the herbs. Repeat the dipping, the sprinkling, and the spell in every room. You may wish to do this once in each room, or to asperge every corner of every room. This is your home and your spell, so that's entirely up to you. If you wish to asperge places such as closets, hallways, and staircases, or things such as a bed, desk, or fireplace—do it. Don't forget the basement, attic, sun room, or attached garage, if your home has any of these.

Work your way deosil through your home, until you are back at your front door. Open it, step outside, and repeat the spell a final time as you draw another pentagram on the exterior of the door.

Go back inside, and ground the power that you raised. You should feel good, and be in a very positive frame of mind. If any water remains in the vessel, return it to the Goddess by pouring it down a drain. Wash the vessel, and discard the ribbon. Rinse the herbs in clear water, and use them fresh or dried in cooking.

Variations
When there is a specific need or problem, customize this spell as required by altering the words "grant blessings to." Variant wordings might include: make happy, bless with love, make secure, bless with health, make prosperous, bless with peace, make harmonious, and so on.

⚘ Abundance Spell ⚘

Abundance is the state of plentitude, of having more than just your basic needs fulfilled. Bread may be the staff of life, but abundance spreads some jam on it. Most cultures have had gods and goddesses who rule abundance, and this spell invokes many of them. You will need:

+ a green candle

+ an orange

+ a piece of bread (A chunk of bread ripped from a fresh loaf is best, but even a slice of commercial bread will work.)

+ a dish of salt

+ your wallet, or whatever you usually keep your money in

Preparation

Cut the orange into quarters. Hold the candle by its wick with your receptive hand. Use your projective hand to slowly rub the orange on it until the whole candle is glistening with juice. Set the candle down in an upright position, and allow it to dry.

The Spell

Gather the spell ingredients. Get into a magickal mood, and create sacred space around the area where you will be working. Focus on abundance, and raise power. Concentrate on what abundance means to you, and what welcome changes it might bring to your life. Remember that abundance takes other forms besides money: an abundance of friends, love, health, or blessings is often more valuable than money.

Place the candle on your altar or other working surface, and position the bread and salt in front of it. Place your wallet to its right. Light the candle. Sprinkle a large pinch of salt over the bread and a smaller pinch over your wallet.

Open your hands and hold them, palms up, on either side of the burning candle. Move your hands gently to direct the smoke from the candle toward yourself as you intone this incantation. Don't worry about pronunciation, and instead concentrate on the power and the beauty of these ancient names as you chant them aloud:

By the bread of Isis
And the salt of Sulis,
By the fruit of Nikkal
And the purse of Cernunnos,
I welcome abundance into my life.
Abundantia, Habondia,
Andarta, Inanna, Rosmerta,
Nehalennia, Nantosuelta,
Damona, Epona, Concordia!
By Inanna's storehouse
And Nehalennia's dog,
By the Dagda's cauldron
And Copia's cornucopia,
Abundantia, Habondia,
Andarta, Inanna, Rosmerta,
Nehalennia, Nantosuelta,
Damona, Epona, Concordia!
I command abundance
To descend upon my life.

abundance come to me
come to me.

Feel the palms of your hands grow warm, and perhaps even perceive a sphere of energy in each hand. Whatever sensation you perceive, name that feeling "abundance," and hold it securely in your memory. Eat the bread and the orange. Concentrate on welcoming abundance while the candle burns all the way down. Feel the energy of the spell entering you with the food and becoming a part of you.

When the candle is spent, ground the power that you raised. You should feel good after casting this spell, energized and in a positive mood. Clean up, and discard the remains of the candle.

Afterward

Don't expect instant results, such as winning the lottery the week after you cast the spell. This is a spell that works through you and brings material improvement in your circumstances because it changes your attitude and your expectations. In the months that follow your casting this spell, you should begin to see improvements that gradually create more comfort in your life.

To keep the spell's magick flowing, eat some bread and salt and oranges from time to time while focusing on making abundance welcome in your life. Keep bright the memory of the feeling that you named "abundance." Open your hands to the Universe, palms up, and accept blessing.

⁓ Chalice of Fertility Spell ⁓

Fertility can apply to human beings, plants, animals, ideas, creativity, plans, businesses, and anything else that has the ability to grow or reproduce. Whether you call her Danu, Allat, Cybele, Isis, Ishtar, Demeter, Anahita, Inanna, or another of her many names, the Great Mother Goddess is the prime deity who rules fertility. Use this spell to invoke her blessing upon anyone or anything that would benefit from more fertility— but only on a person who has requested magickal assistance.

The spell can be cast any time there is reasonably good weather. You will need:

+ coconut milk (Cow's milk may be substituted.)
+ a chalice (Any goblet will do, but one dedicated to magickal usage is best.)
+ a stick of your favorite incense

Preparation

Spend time with the Moon on three consecutive nights. As you gaze at the Moon, meditate on the Mother Goddess and the many blessings that she provides for human beings and our planet. You need to feel close to the Mother in order for this spell to work, so do this for more than three nights if you need to.

The Spell

Get into a magickal mood. Fill the chalice with coconut milk and take it outside. Light the incense and stick it in the ground. Raise power, and create sacred space around the area where you will be working.

Concentrate on the Mother, and on drawing her blessings to you. Pour a libation of coconut milk on the bare ground, as you say:

> Your love is poured out upon the earth.
> Great Mother, please bless _____.

Fill in the blank with whatever you wish to have blessed with fertility. It might be "my loins," "her womb," "this orchard," "our company," or whatever describes your specific intent. You can pour out the whole libation in one place, or offer it in various places as you repeat the spell.

Remain in the place where you poured the libation until the incense finishes burning. Don't allow anything to break your magickal mood as you visualize the power of fertility working in the place or person you have focused it toward. Ground the power that you raised after the incense burns itself out.

Afterward

Wait patiently but expectantly for the spell to manifest. Regard the Moon whenever possible, and smile with the secret knowledge that your spell is at work.

⁓ Ode to Joy Spell ⁓

Joy is the state beyond happiness, an exhilarating lightness-of-being, total body and mind sensation that takes you beyond your ordinary self. It may be hard to recall it sometimes, but we have all experienced joy. This spell helps you to remember what it felt like to be transported by joy, to recapture that feeling, and to keep it close to you. You will need:

+ an orange candle

+ amber or jasmine incense

+ a recording of Beethoven's Ninth Symphony (If you do not care for this piece of music, or cannot obtain it, substitute another for it. Choose a song or other piece of music that is joyful to you.)

The Spell

Get into a magickal mood, and burn the candle while listening to the symphony. Create sacred space for the working. Raise power. Meditate on your joys and sorrows with your focus on all that is or has ever been joyful to you. Recall the most joyous moments of your life and exactly how you felt while experiencing them. Visualize that feeling as a crystal, a ray of light, or whatever image makes sense to you. Hold on to it tightly. Keep it next to your heart, and in your mind.

Light the incense from the candle when the "Ode to Joy" (the operatic part of the symphony) begins. Allow yourself to be flooded with joy as you listen to the soaring music. Visualize the music and the incense smoke undulating around your feeling of joy, entwining with it, and fusing with it. Be one with that feeling. If you are moved to cry, dance, sing, shout, or do something else, go ahead and do it.

Enjoy the music until it ends. Visualize taking the feeling of joy and putting it in a safe place, such as a crystal cave or a secret garden, from which you can retrieve it any time you like. When the joy has been safeguarded, extinguish the candle, and ground the power that you raised.

You should feel great, jazzed up, and energized after casting this spell. Have something to eat or drink to help ground yourself, if you have trouble returning to ordinary consciousness.

Afterward

You may need to repeat the spell many times to achieve this, but at some point your association of the sound of that piece of music, the smell of that incense, and the sight of that color candle burning will become one with your memory of joy. When this happens, any one of them will become a trigger that enables you to feel your joy.

◄ Protective Shield of Janus ◄

Janus (pronounced Jayn-us or Yayn-us) is the double-faced Roman god of beginnings and endings. His dominion includes entrances, exits, thresholds, the first day of each month, and the first day of the year. January, the first month of the year, is named for him. He can be invoked to protect portals, passages, perimeters, people, and property. Be reasonable in your expectations of what the spell can do, though. Placing a psychic shield of protection around your home does not mean that you can then safely leave doors unlocked, ignore needed repairs, or do anything foolish.

This protection spell can be cast at any time, but it is most powerfully cast at dawn or dusk on the first day of a month. You will need:

+ four rocks of the same approximate size (They need to have shapes that will allow images of Janus to be drawn on both sides of each rock and be shaped so that both sides are visible when they are set down. Smooth rocks will be easier to work with. Use larger rocks if you will be placing them outdoors and smaller ones if you will be using them indoors.)

+ a permanent felt-tip pen

+ *Optional*: grains of wheat (bulgur, wheat germ, sprouted wheat, or even wheat flour would do) mixed with salt (Kosher salt, sea salt, or rock salt is best, but ordinary table salt is fine.)

Preparation

Janus is usually depicted as a mature man with short curly hair and a curly beard. Draw his face in profile (as on a coin) on both sides of each rock. Make a left-facing image on one side and a right-facing image on the other. Your artistic ability or accuracy in depicting Janus isn't important; the power of your intent is. As you draw each image say aloud, "This is Janus." Mean it when you say it. Believe it, and it will be Janus.

Put the rocks on your altar or in some other place of honor. Wheat and salt are a traditional offering to Janus. If you are using them, mix them together, and work deosil to spread them around the rocks as an offering.

Next, decide where to place the rocks to create your shield. They could be positioned indoors in the four corners of your house or apartment, or they could be placed outdoors at the four corners of your house, yard, or property. Select four spots to position the rocks. The locations should represent the cardinal points as closely as possible. You can do this mentally, or by physically locating the positions.

The Spell

Get into a magickal mood, and collect the rocks. Create sacred space around them, yourself, and the area where you will be working. Raise power. Focus on Janus until you feel a connection with him. Speak to him in your mind, and ask him to charge the rocks with his powers of protection. Handle the rocks while you do this. Concentrate on charging them until you can almost perceive them glowing or vibrating with power. Hold your hands over them and say:

> *Powers of Janus, powers of rock,*
> *Through the year, around the clock,*
> *Protect us better than a lock.*
> *Powers of Janus, powers of stone,*

Across, about, between, together, alone,
Protect all that is our own.

When the rocks are sufficiently charged, begin placing them in the positions that you have chosen for them. Repeat the words of the spell continuously while you do this. As soon as you place the second rock, visualize a force field or laser light (or whatever image works for you) shooting between the first and second rocks. Build this image as you place the rest of the rocks until the force field covers the entire perimeter, exterior or interior, of your home or property. If the rocks have been placed outdoors, gather up the wheat and salt and sprinkle them over the stones as an offering to Janus. Ground the power that you raised.

Afterward

To keep this spell activated, periodically renew your visualization of the force field. Tend the rocks from time to time by dusting them, clearing leaves or snow from them, or doing whatever is needed to keep the images of Janus visible.

⁓ Seven Blessings Witch's Bottle ⁓

Different witches have different ways of making witch's bottles for various magickal purposes. This is the type of bottle that I make, one that attracts positive energies to the home. Whether you make one of these bottles for yourself, or make several and give the rest as gifts, for each one you will need:

+ a bottle with a tight-fitting cork or cap
+ a pentacle or pentagram (Any type will do, even the symbol ⊗ drawn on a piece of paper.)
+ a white candle
+ white sugar
+ white salt

+ herbs for each of seven blessings (See below.
  Rosemary corresponds to all of the blessings, so it
  may be substituted for any or all of them.)
+ a spoon or funnel

Preparation

Gather all of the spell materials. Get into a magickal mood,
and create sacred space around the area where you will be working. Focus on the blessings you want the bottle to attract to the
home and to those who live there.

Fill the bottle one-third full with salt. Use a spoon to fill
a bottle with a wide opening or a funnel to fill one with a
narrow neck. Tap the bottle a bit on your altar or other working surface to firmly settle the salt.

Add at least one spoonful of one or more dried herbs for
each of these seven blessings: health, happiness, love, prosperity, peace, protection, and good fortune. Add several spoon-
fuls of each herb if you are using a large bottle. Be sure to use
only thoroughly dried herbs, so that they do not ruin your
witch's bottle by spoiling. Add the herbs carefully, so that they
form distinct layers. Any ingredients that are too large to pass
through your bottle's neck may be ground, shattered, chopped,
or reduced in size in another way.

Use whichever herbs correspond to these blessings in your
mind, culture, or magickal tradition. Alternately, use herbs
from the following list of correspondences:

Health: caraway seeds, eucalyptus leaves, ginger, juniper
berries, pine needles, rose hips, sunflower petals or
seeds, thyme

Happiness: baby's breath, cedar chips or shavings, fir
needles, marigold petals, marjoram, orange peel,
oregano, savory

Love: cardamom pods or ground cardamom, carnation
petals, cinnamon chips or ground cinnamon, coriander

seeds, hibiscus flowers, linden flowers, mint, rose petals, willow leaves or bark

Prosperity: acorns, allspice, almonds, banana chips, cloves, oak leaves, oats, poppy seeds, rice, saffron threads, sage

Peace: basil, catnip, lavender, lemongrass, olive branches or leaves, rosemary, violets

Protection: angelica, black beans, cactus needles, garlic powder or garlic salt, nettles, ground black pepper or black peppercorns, thistles, thorns

Good Fortune: ash leaves, bay leaves, cumin seeds or powdered cumin, dill seeds or leaves, whole or ground nutmeg, vanilla beans

Concentrate on each blessing as you add the herb that will attract it to the bottle. Visualize the bottle's magickal power building as each ingredient is added.

Each bottle will be unique. Yours might, for example, have a layer of green eucalyptus leaves on top of the salt. There might be a layer of mixed orange peels and marigold petals atop that, with a layer of rose petals on top of it. A layer of ground sage might come next, then a layer of lavender. They might be followed by layers of black peppercorns and powdered cumin. It is also possible that your bottle might contain nothing but a thick layer of rosemary between the salt and the sugar, or have a rosemary branch in its center, with the salt and sugar poured around it.

Use whatever herbs are available to you. If you have a wide selection, create a bottle that is pleasing to your eye as well as magickally powerful. The bottle should be at least half full when you finish adding the herbs.

Pour sugar over the herbs until the bottle is completely filled. Tap it a few times to help the sugar settle, and add more if needed. Handle the bottle carefully, so that the herbs remain

in layers as much as possible. Close the bottle. Cover it tightly
to seal in the magick, and place it in the center of the pentacle.
Position the candle at the top point of the pentacle.

The Spell

Raise power, and light the candle. Wrap your hands around
the bottle, and charge it with the power of your intent. Clearly
visualize the blessings that the bottle is meant to attract. Pick
up the candle, and begin to drip its wax over the top of the
bottle, as you say:

> *With health and happiness, enchanted be.*
> *With love and prosperity, enchanted be.*
> *With peace and protection, enchanted be.*
> *With good fortune, enchanted be.*
> *Whether placed in house or yard,*
> *Make life better, and less hard.*

Keep dripping wax over the top of the bottle until the candle
is spent. Allow the wax to form a thick seal over the bottle's
opening and to drip down its sides. The bottle should look
very witchy by the time you finish.

Once the wax has hardened, bury the bottle in the yard or
secrete it inside the house. The back of a closet near the front
door is a good indoor place to put it. If you have a large potted
plant, you could bury the bottle in its soil. Keep the bottle in
an upright position, so that the layers of herbs will not mix
together too much. While you bury or hide the bottle, say
repeatedly:

> *Make life better, and less hard.*

Ground power after the bottle is buried or hidden, and clean up.

Afterward

Renew the bottle's magick from time to time by focusing on it
and saying, "Blessed be this home with health, happiness, love,

prosperity, peace, protection, and good fortune." Say this aloud if you are alone or mentally if others are present.

Should you move, you will have to decide what to do with the witch's bottle. A buried bottle can be left behind to bless the new inhabitants of the home, or it can be unearthed and taken with you to your new home. A bottle that was not buried should be taken with you or emptied and discarded. Moving a bottle will ruin its neat layers of herbs, but that will not diminish its magickal potency. Recast the spell if you install an old bottle in a new home.

Variations

This same technique can be used to make many different kinds of witch's bottles. You could make one to attract different blessings by using herbs or charms that correspond to those blessings. If a certain blessing is particularly sought, such as healing, you could make a bottle whose herbs all correspond to that blessing.

⁂ Seven Blessings Bouquet Garni ⁂

A *bouquet garni* is a small bundle of herbs that is added to a soup or stew while it cooks to flavor it and then removed. A magickal bouquet garni will draw its blessings to everyone who eats the food it was cooked in. To make one you will need:

- ✦ a six-inch square of new cheesecloth
- ✦ kitchen string
- ✦ 1 tsp each of the following fresh or dried herbs: thyme (for health), marjoram or savory or oregano (for happiness), coriander seeds (for love), sage (for prosperity), basil or rosemary (for peace), black peppercorns (for protection), and a bay leaf (for good fortune)

Preparation

Gather all of the spell ingredients. Get into a magickal mood, and create sacred space around the area where you will be working. Place the cheesecloth flat on your working surface, and put one spoonful of each herb in its center. While you do this, focus on the blessings that each herb will attract and say:

> *With health and happiness, enchanted be.*
> *With love and prosperity, enchanted be.*
> *With peace and protection, enchanted be.*
> *With good fortune, enchanted be.*
> *Simmered in soup or another food,*
> *Let all who eat it receive good.*

Gather the corners of the cheesecloth and form it into a bundle around the herbs. Tie it tightly with the string.

A bouquet garni made with fresh herbs should be used immediately. One made with dried herbs has the same shelf life as its contents, so any number of these may be made at the same time and stored in an airtight container for future use. It's best to experiment with the herbs a bit to find the mixture whose flavor is most pleasing to you before making a lot of bouquets garnis.

The Spell

Prepare your stew, soup, or other long-simmered dish as usual. Raise power when you turn the burner on below it, and add the bundle of herbs to the pot. Stir it deosil a few times as you concentrate on enchanting the food with the magick of the seven blessings.

Ground power, and continue cooking as usual. Remove the bouquet garni before serving, and discard it.

⁓ Weaving Prosperity Spell ⁓

A spell alone cannot create prosperity, of course. You must work hard and be sensible about your finances, as well as using magick. This spell, along with that ethic, can help you to have a more prosperous life. It invokes Anath, a Middle Eastern goddess who has dominion over prosperity, weaving, and many other things.

The spell is best cast on a Sunday in sunlight. Male or female, if you are comfortable with wearing heavy make-up, you can increase your ability to invoke Anath by wearing it while you cast the spell. Rouge, red lipstick, and black eyeliner are particularly appropriate. You will need:

+ three lengths of gold cord or yarn, each three feet long (Metallic gold is best, but gold-colored cord or yarn will do.)

+ three lengths of green cord or yarn, each three feet long

+ three lengths of orange cord or yarn, each three feet long

+ a green candle, preferably bayberry-scented

+ a purse, or something to represent a purse

+ a stick of cinnamon, cedar, or patchouli incense

+ any prosperity charms that you can obtain, such as green stones, gold coins, orange peels, cedar chips, cinnamon sticks, eagle or dove feathers, money, allspice berries, cloves, cumin seeds, elderberries, balsam fir needles or cones, High John the Conqueror root, juniper berries, bay leaves, whole nutmegs, acorns or oak leaves, pinecones or pineneedles, ears of wheat, cowrie shells, copper rings, or whatever represents prosperity to you (Use dried herbs, not fresh ones.)

The Spell

Repeat this incantation continuously, from the time that you raise power until you ground it:

> Lady Anatha, Queen of Heaven, Strength of Life,
> Help me weave this spell.
> Queen Anath, Ruler of Dominion, Mother of the Gods,
> Charge these cords with power.
> Anatha Baetyl, Lady of the Mountain, Mistress of the Sky,
> Grant me prosperity!

Put all of the spell materials on your altar or other working surface, and get into a magickal mood. Create sacred space around the area where you will be working. Light the candle, and raise power. Meditate on prosperity, and what form you would like it to take in your life.

Focus on that thought as you take the gold cords, knot the three together at one end, and drip some candle wax over the knot to seal it. When the wax has hardened, braid the cords. If you are using any charms that could easily be woven into the braid, add them. Knot the end of the braid, and seal that knot with more candle wax.

Repeat this same procedure with the green cords, and then with the orange ones. When you finish you will have three braids of different colors that are knotted and sealed with green wax on both ends.

Light the incense from the candle. Hold the braids in the smoke, one by one, as you chant the incantation. Concentrate on your concept of prosperity while you do this, and charge the braids with the power to draw prosperity to you.

Braid the three braids together into one thick braid, and seal both its ends with candle wax. While the wax hardens, hold the purse in the incense smoke. Continue to concentrate on drawing prosperity to you.

Put the braid and your prosperity charms into the purse. It should be so full that nothing else will fit in it. Close the purse, and seal it shut with candle wax. Hold it in the incense smoke while you chant the incantation, until you feel that it is fully charged as a prosperity charm.

Place the purse beside the candle, and monitor the candle until it burns itself out. Ground the power that you raised, then, and clean up. Put the purse in a safe place where it will be readily available to you.

Afterward

Handle the purse daily, while focusing on creating prosperity, until its magick begins to manifest. Take it out whenever you need, after that, to encourage or maintain prosperity in your life.

Pillar Candle Spells

Pillar candles are tall, wide, and generally round. They last a long time, so they are excellent for ongoing spells. The way that pillar candles burn varies according to shape, content, and manufacture, but they generally burn down the center. This creates a growing ring of wax around the wick. You may find it necessary with some pillar candles to trim or pour off their wax after you extinguish them, in order to keep their wicks exposed.

The longevity of some pillar candles can be increased by gently pushing the ring of wax inward, while it is warm and malleable, so that the excess wax will be remelted. With time and practice, you will develop a personal method for working with pillar candles.

Many witches feel that to blow out a candle is to extinguish its magick, or to undo the spell. If you feel this way, you should use a candle snuffer for these spells.

~ Healthy Clan Spell ~

Who constitutes your clan? Whose health and well-being is important to you? Does your clan only include close family members, or does it encompass friends, pets, neighbors, colleagues, distant relatives, or others?

Whomever your clan includes, this spell is for all of you. Be realistic in your expectations of it, though. It will encourage wellness, but it will not prevent your clan members from ever falling ill or getting injured.

You can use this spell whenever you like, but it is best cast in sunshine. Charge the candle the first time on a Sunday or on a sunny day while the Moon is waxing (the period between New Moon and Full Moon; use a calendar to determine this). You will need:

+ a large green pillar candle (If you use a scented candle, try make it one with an herbal or evergreen fragrance.)

+ some olive oil

+ a carving tool

+ *Optional*: dried life everlasting flowers

Preparation

Meditate, and determine who the members of your clan are.

The Spell

When you are ready, gather the spell materials, and get into a magickal mood. Create sacred space around the area where you will be working. Carve the name of each clan member into the candle. Don't forget to carve your own name, as well. If you are able to do this, also carve an image of a serpent or the right Eye of Horus 👁 into the candle.

Brush the candle off, and anoint it with the olive oil. Rub it from the top to the middle, and then from the bottom to the middle, until the entire candle has been dressed. Hold the candle by its wick, and place it upright on your altar, or wherever you plan to keep it. If you are using life everlasting flowers, work deosil to arrange them around the base of the candle after the oil has dried.

Raise power, and light the candle. Concentrate on focusing positive, life-giving solar energy into it. If it helps your visualization, stand in sunshine while you do this. Regard the candle and say:

> *Power of light,*
> *Candle burn bright.*
> *As it glows,*
> *Our health grows.*

Visualize the candle's energy reaching each person whose name has been inscribed upon it. When your visualization is complete, and you feel that the candle is properly charged, extinguish it, and ground the power that you raised.

You can light the candle daily, or whenever you wish to send positive energy to the members of your clan. Each time that you light it, say:

> *By the power of the Sun,*
> *I wish good health for everyone.*

Allow the candle to burn as long as feels necessary to you, and then extinguish it.

Afterward

To renew this candle's magick, place it in the Sun for a few hours, and then re-anoint it with olive oil.

⸰ Wings of Isis Spell ⸰

Learning about Isis is a great way to begin this protection spell. She is an active, benevolent deity who answers human prayers. Isis, The Mighty Lady, is also a powerful guardian.

Be realistic about your expectations of what "protection" means. Use common sense. Invoking Isis does not mean that you can now stop wearing your seatbelt, or safely take chances that you know are dangerous. Isis will protect you, but you must also protect yourself.

You can use this spell regularly to keep yourself protected, or you can cast it whenever you feel that it is needed. It requires:

+ a large pillar candle in one of the colors of Isis: sky blue, red, white, or black (If you use a scented candle, try to make it myrrh or rose.)

+ a carving tool

+ *Optional*: some flaxseed oil

+ *Optional*: an image of Isis with her wings outspread

Preparation

Gather the components of the spell. Get into a magickal mood, and create sacred space around the area where you will be working. Carve an ankh ($\female$), one of the symbols of Isis, into the candle. Brush the candle off. If you are using flaxseed oil, rub the candle with it, and allow it to dry.

The Spell

Hold the candle in your hands, and focus your thoughts on Isis. If you have trouble visualizing her, use a picture or a statue of her. Meditate on Isis until you can feel her strength or loving presence.

Raise power, and concentrate on drawing her power into the candle. If it helps your visualization, picture a miniature Isis with her wings wrapped around the candle. When you feel that the candle is properly empowered, light it and say:

Isis with me in the light,
Isis with me in the night,
Goddess mighty, Goddess mild,
Wings protect me, your child.

Remain with the candle, and allow it to burn for a while, as you visualize Isis standing with you and placing you under her protection. You should almost feel her beautiful wings enfolding you protectively. If you have a particular fear or concern, speak to Isis as you would to any respected elder, and ask her to guard you against it. When your visualization is complete, extinguish the candle and ground the power that you raised.

Repeat this spell daily, or whenever you feel frightened or threatened, or any time that you would like to cast it.

Afterward

Rather than using words, offer deeds to thank Isis for her protection. She is a mother goddess, so a good way to thank her is to do something kind for children. Watch out for the safety of every child you encounter, or volunteer to read to kids, or donate time or money to a children's organization, or help children in some other way.

⋅⁓ Incense Ritual ⁓⋅

This is a very simple ritual that can be performed any time, anywhere. You can use it daily, or whenever you feel the need for it. The ritual grows more powerful as it is repeated. It draws positive energies to you, protects you from evil and danger, and helps with centering and balancing. You will need:

✦ a stick of incense, in any scent that appeals to you

The Ritual

Light the incense. Be mindful of fire safety when performing this ritual, and watch out for falling sparks. With a sweeping gesture, inscribe ☆ in the air as you declare,

With this incense,
I draw all that is fair!

Then inscribe a downward-pointing star in the same manner, as you declare,

> With this incense,
> I banish all that is negative!

If you find it difficult to draw stars in the air, you can instead swirl the incense deosil the first time and widdershins the second time. When you finish, put the incense into a holder, and allow it to burn down completely.

Variations

This ritual can be adapted in many ways. If you like, you can face each of the cardinal points in turn, starting with East or North, and repeat it. You could also move through your residence (or hotel room, or wherever you happen to be) and repeat the ritual at every window and door, or repeat it wherever you feel would be a good place to perform it. If you have a particular thought, special wish, or issue, you can include it—with the invoking star or the banishing one, as the case may be.

⚬ Personal Blessings Ritual ⚬

This ritual has two purposes: to give thanks for the blessings that you already have and to draw additional blessings into your life. As with all rituals, the more often that it is performed, the stronger, more effective, and more meaningful it becomes.

This is not a fixed, immutable ritual; it is one that you can create anew each time that you perform it, by incorporating whatever blessings are present or needed at the time. You can enact the Blessings Ritual whenever you like, but it is best performed on sunny days. You will need:

+ one bay leaf (laurel) for each blessing (You can find bay leaves where spices are sold. Offerings should be as perfect as possible, so try to use only whole leaves that do not have blemishes or broken edges. If you

cannot obtain bay leaves, other kinds of leaves may
be substituted.)

+ honey

+ a container, something flat that can easily be
transported to the offering site, such as a tray or a
shallow basket or box

+ a river, stream, or other watercourse (Adapt the
ritual to your location. If you live in a desert, you
could instead bury your offerings in the sand; if you
live in a frozen place, you could give your offerings
to the wind; if you live at the seaside, you could
instead offer them to the ocean, and so on.)

+ a bridge or other location from which you can safely
make offerings

+ *Optional*: additional offerings (See below.)

Preparation

Count your blessings. What are you grateful for? Good health,
prosperity, freedom, family . . . a list of our blessings will be different for each of us, according to the circumstances of our lives.

Next, identify two or three blessings that you would like to
ask the gods for. Be reasonable about this. Most of us would love
to win a major lottery jackpot, but it is more realistic to request
abundance, prosperity, or a good job.

Once you know how many blessings will be incorporated
into your ritual, assemble that number of leaves and the honey.
Get into a magickal mood, and create sacred space around the
area where you will be working. Honey is messy, so it's best to
use the kitchen for this part of the ritual.

Lay out the bay leaves on the container. Spoon or drip
some honey into the center of each leaf. As you dress a leaf
with honey, name aloud the blessing for which that leaf will be
offered.

Optional: Offerings

You can increase the magickal power of your ritual by incorporating offerings—herbs, seeds, flower petals, or other natural charms—for each blessing sought. To do this, stick an appropriate charm into the honey on the leaf that represents that blessing.

You are going to offer the leaves by tossing them into moving water (or otherwise leaving them outdoors). It would defeat the purpose of the ritual to do something that might damage the environment or cause harm to creatures, so the charms should be nontoxic and biodegradable as well as small enough to fit on the leaves.

Rosemary and cinnamon are herbs that have many magickal associations, so you could simply sprinkle either or both of them on each leaf before offering it. Alternately, you could add pink, yellow, or orange flower petals for attraction to the leaves that represent those blessings you hope to draw with the ritual.

If you would like to be more precise with your offerings, the following are examples of natural charms that have magickal correspondence to some typical blessings. There are a great many other herbal charms, but this list concentrates on commonplace ones. Several choices are given for each blessing whenever possible, but one type of charm per offering is sufficient.

Abundance: orange peel, raw popcorn kernels
Advancement: red leaf, red flower petals
Beauty: jasmine, lavender, lily, orchid, or rose petals
Comfort: cloves, fir tips, marjoram, sage
Courage: garlic, black pepper, black tea
Fertility: banana chips, dark blue flower petals, peach pit, pine nuts or pineneedles, rice, wheat flour

Fidelity: cumin seeds or powdered cumin, chili pepper, a drop of hot sauce

Freedom: bird of paradise or lily petals

Friendship: drop of aloe juice, pink carnation petals, geranium leaf or petals, ivy leaf, lemon zest

Good Fortune: dill seeds, mint, pomegranate seeds, poppy seeds, a drop of pure vanilla extract

Good Health: acorn, apple peel, ginseng, marjoram, nutmeg

Good Luck: allspice, basil, catnip, clover, cornmeal

Happiness: apple peel, baby's breath, lemon zest, marigold petals, savory, sunflower seeds

Healing: pearl barley, cedar shavings, eucalyptus leaf, lime zest, rose thorn, saffron thread, thyme

Inspiration: hazelnut, purple or violet flower petals

Justice: cedar chips or shavings, pinecones or pineneedles

Longevity: fennel seeds, piece of date or fig, maple syrup, pollynose (maple tree seed), sage

Love: chamomile, ginseng, hibiscus, jasmine, lavender, red rose petals, willow leaf or bark

Loyalty: blue flower petals, lime zest, rosemary

Patience: azalea leaf or flower, chamomile, iris petals

Peace: chamomile flowers, lavender, lemongrass, drop of olive oil, white rose petals

Popularity: angelica, grape, drop of passionflower juice

Prosperity: allspice, cloves, nutmeg, sage, tangerine peel

Protection: birch bark, garlic, pepper, kosher salt, nettles, thistles, thorns, drop of witch hazel

Strength: red or orange carnation petals, garlic

Success: allspice berry, cinnamon, orange or purple flower petals, ginger, lemon balm

Truth: chrysanthemum petals, white flower petals

Victory: fennel seeds, piece of palm frond

Warmth: cactus needles, coriander seeds, Japanese maple
   leaf, marigold petals, mesquite chip
Wealth: acorn, almond, basil, moss, saffron threads

The Ritual

Take the prepared leaves to the offering site that you have
selected. Raise power and reverently cast them, one by one,
into the moving water. As you offer each leaf, say:

> To (*name of deity*), for (*blessing*).

You can invoke your matron goddess, your patron god, or any
other deities that you like. You can also make the invocations
more general, such as:

> To Mother Earth, for rain.
> To the Lord and the Lady, for love.
> To the Goddess, for prosperity.
> To the Corn Mother, for abundance.
> To all the gods, for peace.

Concentrate on your intent as you make each offering. When
giving thanks for a blessing, focus on the gratitude that you
feel for its presence in your life. When working to attract a blessing, focus on your need or desire for that blessing.

Optional: Invocation

The numinous power of your ritual can be increased by invoking specifically appropriate deities for the blessings, as in the
following examples. Don't worry about mispronouncing their
names. They will know whom you mean and that you mean
well by calling upon them.

Celtic: To Sulis, for good health. To Brigid, for healing. To
   Angus, for love. To Epona, for abundance. To Rhiannon,
   for truth. To Cliodna (pronounced "kleena"), for beauty.
   To Aine (pronounced "aw ne"), for prosperity. To the
   Dagda, for protection. To Maeve, for strength. To

Cernunnos, for good fortune. To the Morrigan, for justice. To Danu, for all blessings.

Egyptian: To Isis, for peace. To Hathor, for love. To Bast, for abundance. To Khonsu, for fertility. To Renenutet, for good fortune. To Neith, for protection. To Ma'at, for justice. To Sesheta, for patience. To Sekhmet, for healing. To Ra, for strength. To Thoth, for success. To Selket, for a good marriage. To Bes, for a happy home. To Nephthys, for protecting the household. To Osiris, for all blessings.

Greek: To Atalanta, for courage. To Aphrodite, for love. To Hygeia, for good health. To Zeus, for protection. To Apollo, for healing. To Nike, for victory. To Dike, for justice. To Hades, for wealth. To Helios, for warmth. To Rhea, for abundance. To Aega, for beauty. To Philotes, for friendship. To the Muses, for inspiration. To Hermes, for lucky breaks. To Demeter, for prosperity. To Eirene, for peace. To Gaia, for a happy marriage. To Hestia, for a peaceful home life. To the Graces, for gracious living. To Pandora, for all blessings.

Mesopotamian: To Inanna, for abundance. To Gula, for good health. To Geshtinanna, for love. To Dazimus, for healing. To Marduk, for victory. To Shamash, for truth. To Kadi, for justice. To Aya, for all blessings.

Native American (including Aztec, Incan, and Mayan): To Catheña, for love. To Chie, for happiness. To Glispa, for healing. To Fura-Chogue, for peace. To Xochiquetzal, for beauty. To Maximón, for success. To Deohako, for abundance. To Tlaloc, for fertility. To Tonantzin, for good health. To Ukat, for good luck. To Pachamama, for good fortune. To Hanwi, for comfort. To Salmon Woman, for protection. To Copper Woman, for wealth. To Otter Woman, for fun. To Chantico, for protecting the home. To Changing Woman, for all blessings.

Norse: To Thor, for strength. To Odin, for victory. To Freya, for longevity. To Sjofna, for love. To Fulla, for abundance. To Njord, for wealth. To Heimdall, for protection. To Forseti, for justice. To Baldur, for popularity. To Eir, for healing. To Gonlod, for inspiration. To Tyr, for courage. To Gerd, for fertility. To Hlin, for comfort. To Sigyn, for loyalty. To Vara, for fidelity. To Gefion, for good fortune.

Roman: To Amor, for love. To Diana, for strength. To Venus, for beauty. To Minerva, for peace. To Pluto, for prosperity. To Liber, for fertility. To Mercury, for healing. To Jupiter, for justice. To Jupiter Victor, for victory. To Neptune, for protection. To Mars Ollodius, for abundance. To Juno, for a prosperous marriage. To Vesta, for a happy home and a stable marriage. To Acca Larentia, for material blessings. To the Lares, for protecting the household. To the Penates, for safeguarding the family.

Closing

When you finish making your offerings, stand quietly for a few moments. You are in the presence of the gods you have invoked, so this is a good time to commune with them in any way that feels natural to you. You can ask for answers or guidance as well as blessings, if you like.

Focus on the blessings. Feel them around you, or approaching you. Give thanks to the gods for your blessings and for accepting your offerings. Ground the power that you raised, and take whatever you used to carry the blessings away with you.

⸮ King of Peace Seven-Day Spell ⸝

This spell creates a charm that you can keep near you to promote peace in every aspect of yourself and in every area of your life. It invokes Obatala, The Old Man of the Mountain, an

African god who is considered a goddess in some traditions. He is known by many names in the New World, including Oxala and Orisha Popo.

Begin the spell on a Saturday at any time of day or night. You will need:

+ two blue or white candles
+ a white cloth
+ eight sticks of patchouli incense (one for each day, plus an extra stick)
+ a blue or white mojo bag
+ a small blue or white stone
+ seven pinches of dried rosemary
+ seven rose petals, preferably from a white rose
+ seven clean, shiny dimes (Seven cowrie shells, seven silver coins, or seven small silver objects could be substituted for the dimes.)
+ *Optional*: an image of Obatala
+ *Optional*: white altar furnishings, including "white" metals such as silver or pewter

DAY ONE

Preparation

Gather all of the spell ingredients. Get into a magickal mood, and create sacred space around the area where you will be working. Spread the white cloth on your altar or other working surface. If you have an image of Obatala, place it nearby. Put one candle and one stick of incense on the cloth. (Reserve the other candle and the rest of the incense for the other days of the spell.)

The Spell

Raise power. Light the candle, then light the incense from it. Hold the stone in your hands. Focus on charging it with peace as you say:

> *Obatala, King of Peace,*
> *Chief of the White Cloth,*
> *Father-Mother of Humanity,*
> *Bringer of Peace and Harmony,*
> *I charge this stone with your positive energy.*
> *Obatala, by your power,*
> *This stone is charged with peace.*

Hold the stone in the incense smoke for a minute. Concentrate on peace and harmony while you do this, then put the stone into the mojo bag. Say one of these blessings for each rose petal, as you hold it in the smoke for a moment and then add it to the bag:

> *For peace with myself.*
> *For peace with my past.*
> *For peace with my present.*
> *For peace with my future.*
> *For peace with my karma.*
> *For peace with those who love me.*
> *For peace with those who do not love me.*

Do the same with the coins, saying a blessing for each one as you hold it in the smoke and then add it to the mojo bag:

> *For peace of mind.*
> *For peace of heart.*
> *For peace of spirit.*
> *For peace at home.*
> *For peace at work (or school).*
> *For peace in the family.*
> *For peace in the world.*

Do the same with each pinch of rosemary, but this time use seven blessings of your own devising. Each line should represent a different area of your life or aspect of yourself in which you wish for peace. You will be very focused on peace by this point in the spell, so the blessings should come easily to you. Speak from your heart, and say whatever comes to mind. You may wish, for example, to name seven people with whom you would like to be at peace. If the incense burns down before you finish, light the extra incense stick from the candle flame and continue.

When everything has been smudged and put into the mojo bag, close it tightly. If possible, tie seven knots in its drawstring. Ground the power you raised. Leave the bag atop the white cloth, and put them in a safe place, where they can remain undisturbed while you work with them during the week.

DAY TWO through DAY SIX

The Spell
Each day, burn a stick of incense on the altar. Hold the mojo bag in its smoke, turning it so that the entire bag is smudged. While you do this, concentrate on peace and say:

> *By the power of the number seven,*
> *By the white clouds in the heavens,*
> *With blessed peace and harmony,*
> *This mojo bag enchanted be!*

DAY SEVEN

The Spell
Do the same on the seventh day, but raise power this time, and light the remaining candle as well as the last stick of incense. After you have smudged the mojo bag, use the candle to drip seven splashes of wax over the knots that close it. As you do this, concentrate on peace and again say:

By the power of the number seven,
By the white clouds in the heavens,
With blessed peace and harmony,
This mojo bag enchanted be!

The spell is complete once the candle and the incense have finished burning. When the wax that seals the knots has hardened, you can put the bag wherever you plan to keep it. Ground the power that you raised, and clean up.

Afterward

If your need for peace is constant, keep this bag with you. Mojo bags are traditionally worn around the neck. You could do that or carry yours in a pocket, handbag, backpack, or briefcase. If lack of peace is a problem mainly in one place, such as at home, school, or your office, you might want to keep the bag there.

If your need for peace is intermittent, you can keep the bag in a safe place and take it out whenever its magick is needed. If it has been stored away for a time, squeeze it a few times to reactivate it. To refresh the bag's magick at any time, smudge it with patchouli incense.

When the issues that brought you to needing this spell are no longer issues, you can consider the spell's work complete. The mojo bag can then be buried, burned, thrown out, put away in a safe place, or disposed of in whatever way seems best to you. The stone and coins or other charms may be cleared (see "stones" under "Spell Ingredients" on page xviii) and retained for future use, if you like.

Chamber Spells

Moving, renovating, or redecorating provides the opportunity to enchant a room. Several chamber spells are given here. These are spirit-of-place workings that improve the energy signatures of rooms in specific ways. The names of the deities invoked will be written on walls and doors, so it will be necessary to paint or wallpaper after casting the spells. That will conceal the Words of Power but not deactivate them.

Please note that it is important to the success of all of these spells that the rooms be completely emptied and thoroughly cleaned before the spells are cast.

◌⸳ Nursery Spell ⸳◌

Preparation for the arrival of a new baby often includes making a bedroom ready. This spell can be used whenever those prepa-rations include painting or wallpapering the room that is to be the nursery. It is best cast by the child's parent(s) but could be cast (with permission) by someone else who cares about the baby. The spell provides extra protection for a baby, but the parent(s) must of course still take normal precautions and take excellent care of the baby in order for this spell to work.

You will need:

+ a pencil or other writing implement (Use a pencil if you will be painting the room, something heavier if you will be putting up wallpaper.)
+ myrrh incense

Preparation

Empty the room completely. Open the window(s) to air it out, and clean the room thoroughly. Be sure to clean any closet(s) as well. Keep scrubbing and sweeping or vacuuming until you feel that the room is devoid of whatever vibrations it previously held.

The Spell

Get into a magickal mood, and create sacred space in the clean room. Bring in the incense, and light it. Envision the nursery as a place of safety and happiness for the baby. Raise power, and pour all your love for the baby into the room. Fill the room with that love, and visualize it being absorbed into the walls, floor, and ceiling.

While the incense burns, inscribe the names of the following gods and goddesses upon the walls. Say each sentence aloud as you write the name of the deity. Change the wording as appropriate for gender, for a multiple birth, or to include the baby's name.

On the door or above the doorway, write: "VOLUMNA, to protect this nursery. PILUMNUS, to guard this baby, from birth until it reaches the safety of this room."

Near the place where the baby will sleep, write: "ARTEMIS, to protect this baby. JUNO, to watch over this baby. DEVERRA, to safeguard this baby. LAIMA, to look after this baby. INTERCIDONA, to keep this baby safe."

On any wall, write: "POTNIA, to make sure this baby is well nourished. BES, to give this baby the gifts of laughter and safety. LUCINA, to protect this baby's eyesight. JUNO LUCINA, to keep this baby healthy. THE ZORYA, to ensure that this baby is always well cared for. THE SEVEN HATHORS, to bless this baby's future."

Remain in the room until the incense finishes burning. (Light another stick or add more myrrh to the censer, if needed.) Look around the room, and feel the difference that your work has made in its spirit of place. Visualize a happy, healthy baby sleeping, laughing, and playing there.

Ground the power that you raised once your visualization is complete, and the incense has burned out. You can now paint or wallpaper the room, and then furnish and decorate it.

⁖ Children's Room Spell ⁖

The bedrooms of children of any age can be enchanted to enhance their happiness and well-being. This spell can be cast for a room where one child sleeps or for a room that is shared by two or more children. It is best cast by the parent(s) but can be cast by anyone who cares about the kids. You will need:

+ pine or rosemary incense

+ a writing implement (Use a pencil if you will be painting the room, something heavier if you will be putting up wallpaper.)

+ *Optional*: a mojo bag that contains vervain (for their happiness and learning ability), a citrine (to protect them from negative influences), chamomile (for their emotional security), and any other charms that you would like to add

Preparation

Empty the room completely. Open the window(s) to air it out, and clean the room thoroughly. Be sure to clean the closet(s), as well as the bathroom if the room has an attached bath. Keep scrubbing and sweeping or vacuuming until you feel that the room has become void of any vibrations that it previously held.

The Spell

Get into a magickal mood, and create sacred space in the clean room. Bring in the incense, and light it. Visualize the bedroom as a place of strength, encouragement, and refuge for the children. Raise power, and pour all your love and hopes for them into the room. Fill the bedroom with that feeling, and visualize it being absorbed into the walls, floor, and ceiling.

While the incense burns, inscribe the names of the following gods and goddesses upon the walls. Change the wording as needed for number and gender, and say each sentence aloud as you write the name of the deity.

On the door or above the doorway, write: "ABEONA, to protect them when they are away from home. ADEONA, to safeguard them at school." Above their beds, write: "CARDEA, to watch over them while they sleep."

Anywhere in the room, write: "ARTEMIS, to protect them. ISIS, to watch over them. SEKHMET, to safeguard them. BAST, to look after them. LEGBA, to ward them. LA SIRENE, to protect them in the tub and shower. KWAN YIN, to keep them safe. JEZANNA, to keep them healthy. SASTHI, for their happiness and welfare. BES, for their laughter. YEMAYA, to comfort them whenever they need comforting."

Remain in the room until the incense finishes burning. (Light another stick or add more to the censer, if needed.) Look around the room, and feel the difference that your work has made in its spirit of place. Envision happy, healthy, well-balanced kids growing up there. If you have made a charm bag, hold it in the incense smoke to smudge it while you do this.

Once your visualization is complete, and the incense has burned out, ground the power that you raised. You can now paint or wallpaper the room, then furnish and decorate it. If you have made a mojo bag, secrete it somewhere in the room, such as under a floorboard or in the back of a closet.

⁓ Kitchen Spell ⁓

The kitchen is the center of a home, so bespelling it can benefit the entire family as well as everyone who eats the food prepared there. This spell is best cast by the person who will do most of the cooking, but it could be cast on behalf of the household (with permission) by someone who cares about them. You will need:

+ an incense of Fire, such as copal, rose, dragon's blood, or frankincense

+ a writing implement (Use a pencil if you will be painting the room, something heavier if you will be putting up wallpaper.)

+ *Optional*: a Kitchen Witch (This is a witch doll, or a ceramic figure of a witch, that is meant to be displayed as a charm in a kitchen. Housewares shops often carry them.)

Preparation

Empty the kitchen of everything except any appliances that are too difficult to move. Open the window(s) to air it out, and clean the room thoroughly. Be sure to clean the cabinets, any cupboards or pantries, as well as any attached area such as a deck or porch. Keep scrubbing and sweeping until you feel that the room is devoid of any vibrations it previously held.

The Spell

Get into a magickal mood, and create sacred space in the kitchen. Bring in the incense, and put it on the stove or in the place where the stove will be. Light it, and raise power. Envision the kitchen as a center of warmth, comfort, love, and nurturing. Raise power, and pour all of those feelings into the room. Visualize it as Magick Central, a place whose positive magnetic energy will draw people to it and foster happy times. Picture the wonderful meals that will be prepared there and how they will nourish people, emotionally as well as physically. Fill the room with those thoughts, and visualize them being absorbed into the walls, floor, cabinets, appliances, and ceiling.

While the incense burns, inscribe the names of the following gods and goddesses upon the walls. Change the wording if needed, and say each sentence aloud as you write the name of the deity. Over the doorway, write: "THE LARES, to protect the household. THE PENATES, to safeguard the family. TSAO-CHÜN, to watch over the family." Above or near the stove, write: "BRIGID, for warmth. THOR, for strength. ERTHA, for abundance. ZEUS, for protection. CHANTICO, for security. DOLYA, for good luck. VESTA, for a happy home. HESTIA, for a peaceful home. ATHENE, for family unity. USHAS, to protect the hearth. KIKIMORA, to keep the house in good order."

Remain in the kitchen until the incense finishes burning. Light another stick or add more to the censer, if needed. If you have a Kitchen Witch, hold it in the incense smoke to smudge it while you look around the room and feel the difference that your work has made in its spirit of place.

Once your visualization is complete and the incense has burned out, ground the power that you raised. You can now paint or wallpaper the kitchen, then move everything into it. If there is a Kitchen Witch, place or hang it where it can be seen from the stove.

⌁ Family Room Spell ⌁

The place in the home where family and friends usually gather, such as a living room, family room, or dining room, has a special energy of its own. To enchant such a room is to touch everyone who frequents it with positive magick.

This spell is best cast by a member of the family, but it could be cast for them (with permission) by someone who cares about them. You will need:

✦ rose, ylang ylang, or dragon's blood incense

✦ a writing implement (Use a pencil if you will be painting the room, something heavier if you will be putting up wallpaper.)

Preparation

Empty the room completely. Open the window(s) to air it out, and clean the room thoroughly. Be sure to clean any closets or fireplaces, as well as any attached area such as a deck, porch, or balcony. Keep scrubbing and sweeping or vacuuming until you feel that the room has become void of any vibrations it previously held.

The Spell

Get into a magickal mood, and create sacred space in the room. Bring in the incense, light it, then raise power. Visualize the room as a place of unity and happiness. Picture your family and friends, all healthy and thriving, gathering together there.

Fill the room with benevolence and positive energy, and visualize it being absorbed into the walls, floor, and ceiling.

While the incense burns, inscribe the names of the following gods and goddesses upon the walls. Change the wording as needed, and say each sentence aloud as you write the name of the deity.

On the door or above the doorway, write: "CARDEA, to protect family life. HESTIA, for a peaceful home life. FRIGG, for the well-being of the family." On any wall write: "DURGA, for family union. VERPLACE, for good family relations. AERTEN, to settle family quarrels. JARA, for a healthy family. MAHA LAKSHMI, for family prosperity. PIETAS, for meeting family responsibilities. THE PENATES, to protect the family."

Remain in the room until the incense finishes burning. (Light another stick or add more to the censer, if needed.) Look around the room, and feel the difference that your work has made in its spirit of place. Once your visualization is complete, and the incense has burned out, ground the power that you raised. You can now paint or wallpaper the room, then furnish and decorate it.

⁓ Master Bedroom Spell ⁓

Use this spell to bespell the bedroom where a married (or otherwise deeply committed) couple sleeps. It is best cast by both partners together but can also be cast by just one of them. You will need:

+ rose or jasmine incense
+ a writing implement (Use a pencil if you will be painting the room, something heavier if you will be putting up wallpaper.)
+ *Optional*: potted ivy, roses, rosemary, violets, or cyclamen

Preparation

Empty the bedroom completely. Open the window(s) to air it out, and clean the room thoroughly. Be sure to clean any closets, bathrooms, hallways, or fireplaces, as well as any attached area such as a deck or balcony. Keep scrubbing and sweeping or vacuuming until you feel that the bedroom (or master suite) is devoid of any vibrations that it previously held.

The Spell

Get into a magickal mood, and create sacred space in the bedroom. Bring in the incense, and light it. Visualize the bedroom as a place that fosters perfect love and perfect trust. Focus on a stable, loving, enduring relationship. Raise power, and pour all your love and hopes for the relationship into the room.

Envision the room as a sanctuary where love will be renewed each time the couple sleeps there. Visualize a bond so strong, and a relationship so satisfying on every level, that none of the vicissitudes of life will ever be able to break the marriage apart. Fill the room with the strength of this conjugal love, and visualize it being absorbed into the walls, floor, and ceiling.

While the incense burns, inscribe the names of the following gods and goddesses upon the walls. Change the wording as needed, and say each sentence aloud as you write the name of the deity.

On the door or above the doorway, write: "BES, to protect this chamber. OSHUN, to safeguard our relationship. SELKET, to preserve our union. VARA, to protect our marriage." Above the bed, write: "PARVATI, to watch over us. FREYA, for a happy marriage. HATHOR, for pleasure in marriage. FRIGG, for great sex in marriage. APHRODITE, for the sanctity of our marriage. ISIS, to protect our love."

On any wall, write: "BENZAITEN, for good fortune. VESTA, for stability. JUNO, for a prosperous marriage. THOR, for a fruitful union. HOLDA, for a proper home. SHEKINAH, for blessings."

Bring the potted plant into the room, if you are using one, and place it near a window. Remain there until the incense finishes burning. Light another stick or add more to the censer, if needed. Look around the bedroom, and feel the difference that your work has made in its spirit of place.

Once your visualization is complete and the incense has burned out, ground the power that you raised. You can now paint or wallpaper the bedroom, then furnish and decorate it.

⋅⁖5⁖⋅

Problem Solving

One of the biggest magickal mistakes that I see people make is to try to rely on magick alone to solve their problems. We have to be responsible and use common sense as well as cast spells, if we expect our magick to succeed.

If you're a smoker, all the good health spells in the world are unlikely to save you from lung diseases. If you smoke near family members, you would do better to stop smoking (or at least stop smoking around them) than to cast protection spells for your family. If you're depressed, you need to see a doctor, not cast a happiness spell. We need to look at ourselves honestly and determine whether or not we are causing our problems. If this is the case, we should do something about it before we turn to magick.

That said, the spells in this chapter can help you deal with everything from tragedy, conflict, obsession, and nightmares to hexes, crossed conditions, invasions of privacy, and more. Don't forget common sense, though, and use ordinary solutions along with the spells.

⁖ Silver Bullet Spell ⁖

Legend has it that a werewolf can only be killed by a silver bullet. Do you have a problem that is so menacing, so fearsome, or so dangerous that it has become almost like a werewolf in your life? Have all nonmagickal efforts to deal with the werewolf failed? If so, this spell can help you. Naturally it is best cast on the night of a Full Moon (use a calendar to time it). Casting it in moonlight, or in view of the Moon, will increase its power.

This is a serious spell that should be reserved for serious problems. Use it wisely. It is designed to eliminate problems, not to do harm to anyone or anything. To misuse this spell is to paint a bull's-eye on yourself and invite three silver bullets to strike you. Proceed with caution.

The spell invokes Diana, a powerful Roman triple goddess whose dominion includes hunting and the Moon. To cast it you will need:

+ a silver candle, preferably metallic silver
+ a carving tool
+ a writing implement
+ a bull's-eye (This is a dark circle with several concentric circles around it, such as is used in archery. You can use an actual bull's-eye or draw one on a piece of paper.)
+ arrowroot powder (This can be found where spices are sold.)
+ *Optional*: items connected with the problem, such as documents or letters

Preparation

Identify your problem. That sounds simple, but it is the most crucial element of the spell. If you do not aim the silver bullet correctly, your spell will go wrong. For instance, you might blame someone else for the problem, when in fact it is your own actions or inactions that have caused it. Or, in a case of infidelity, you might be tempted to target the lover when your partner is the one who should actually be held accountable. In such a case it would probably be better to end the relationship than to use magick to try to end the affair.

Consider everything. Give it deep thought. Try to see the big picture and your place in it. Meditate on the situation, or ask for a dream message about it, if you need to.

When you feel that you have correctly identified your problem, sum it up in one or two words. Write them in the center of the bull's-eye, and carve them into the candle. It's fine if it's hard to see what you have written on the bull's-eye; all that matters is that the words have been written there. If the candle is large enough, also carve the symbol for the triple Moon upon it ( )Ⅾ( ).

Spending time with the Moon, especially on the nights leading up to the Full Moon, is an excellent way to prepare yourself to cast this spell. Focus on your problem, while you commune with the Moon, and on possible ways that it could be solved without any harm being done.

The Spell

Gather the candle, the bull's-eye, and anything else you are using for the spell. Get into a magickal mood, and create sacred space around the area where you will be working. Put the bull's-eye on your altar or other working surface, and place the candle upright in its center. If you are using items that are connected to the problem, place them on the altar. Flat items, such as pictures or documents, can be put under the bull's-eye; anything else can be placed around it.

Working widdershins, spread the arrowroot powder around the candle. Raise power, raise your arms, and say:

Hail Diana!
Queen of Witches,
I call upon thee.
Jana, Tana, Fana,[2]
Please help me.

Touch the candle. Visualize it as a magickal silver bullet that is going to strike your problem and eliminate it. Raise power higher. You should feel magickal tension rising, as if you are pulling hard on a bow to draw an arrow into shooting position. Raise your arms again and say:

Maiden Huntress,
I call upon you
To steady my arm,
Let me do no harm,
And make my aim true.

Light the candle, thereby setting the spell in motion. Say:

Bullet speed, through the dark,
Straight on course, to the source,
Find your target, hit your mark!

Repeat this as many times as you feel is necessary. Concentrate on an image of the silver bullet hurtling through the darkness to strike your problem. If you have raised sufficient power, you should be able to "feel" the impact. Monitor the candle while it burns. Visualize the problem shattering, fading, withering, melting, receding, growing smaller, disappearing, or whatever image best makes sense in the context of your problem. Watch the candle burn, and allow yourself to begin to feel a sense of relief.

---

2. Jana, Tana, and Fana are all old names for Diana.

It's fine if the candle wax runs onto the bull's-eye or mixes with the arrowroot powder. Once the candle has burned out, gather up the powder, and take it outside. Carry it on the bull's-eye, if you like. Face each of the cardinal points in turn. Start with the North, work deosil, and toss or blow one-fourth of the powder in each of the four directions. Each time that you do this, say:

> By candle's light,
> By bullet's flight,
> Queen of the Night,
> Make things right.
> Diana Triformis, goddess trine,
> Let a good solution be mine!

The spell should have raised a lot of power, and by this point you may be feeling the physical effects of it, such as trembling or lightheadedness. Ground the power. Physically touch the earth or hug a tree, if necessary. Go back inside, and clean up. Have something to eat or drink if you are still feeling the effects of the spell.

Afterward

Remember that the more difficult or complicated a problem is, the more complex and time-consuming its solution may be. If you have cast the spell properly, you should see some action toward a solution by the next Full Moon. If nothing happens, or if the problem gets worse, consider that you may have been wrong in your assessment of the situation. Start again. Reconsider the problem, work toward making a more accurate identification of it, and aim a new silver bullet.

⁓ Computer Repair ⁓

Psi-magick can be used to help a computer to repair itself. This works best with computers that you use frequently and have a feel for. It also helps if you, like me, absolutely love your computer.

First, run whatever diagnostic and repair program is recommended for your computer. If that does the trick, great, you don't need a spell. If it didn't solve the problem, shut the computer down, and allow it to rest for a while.

Rub the palms of your hands together, then separate your hands, but continue to make the same motions. This is a basic way to raise magickal power, and you should soon feel it as an energy field between your palms.

Turn the computer back on. Focus on it, and concentrate as it starts up until you can sense the computer's energy field. Restart the diagnostic/repair program, but this time hold your hands over the hard drive while the program runs. Focus your whole attention on channeling the energy in your hands to the computer and on helping it to repair itself. Enjoy the sensation of feeling yourself joining with the machine and working in sync with it.

Ground the power that you raised as soon as the computer notifies you that it has repaired itself.

Cool-Down Spells

⁓ Cooling Attraction ⁓

Do you lust for someone who is already taken or absolutely wrong for you? Are you suffering from unrequited love? Is there someone you need to get over, so that you can move on with your life? Do you have an unhealthy obsession with someone? Are you finally ready to end a toxic relationship? If that sounds like you, this spell can help.

You will need:

+ a poppet of yourself (This could be anything from a sewn "voodoo doll" to a chess piece. Anything that represents you, in your mind, will do nicely. Something heart-shaped, to represent your heart, would also make a good poppet for this spell. If the attraction is more physical than emotional, you could instead use something to represent your phallus or vulva, as appropriate.)

+ a pen or marker that will write on the poppet

+ a cup of unsweetened lemon balm tea (*Melissa officinalis*)

+ a sealable plastic bag that is big enough to hold the poppet

+ your freezer

Preparation

Get into a magickal mood, and create sacred space around the area where you will be working. If your attraction is to a woman, inscribe the poppet with this female symbol: ♀. If your attraction is to a man, inscribe the poppet with this male symbol: ♂.

Make a cup of lemon balm tea. Be mindful, as you brew the tea, that indifference—not hatred—is the opposite of love. Do not add sweetener to the tea. Drink half of it, and allow the other half to sit until it becomes lukewarm.

The Spell

Raise power. Hold the poppet in your projective hand. Command it to "get real" about the person and about the situation. Put the poppet into the plastic bag, and pour the lukewarm tea over it. It isn't a problem if this causes the ink of the symbol to run.

Seal the bag, and put it into your freezer. Stick it out of the way in a place where it will not be seen every time the freezer is opened. Visualize your feelings for this person freezing with the tea. Tell yourself that your feelings will not thaw so long as the poppet is in the freezer. Repeat this assurance as many times as needed until you are convinced the spell will work, then ground the power that you raised.

Afterward

Whenever you have any contact with this person, summon the feeling of ice water into your veins as you deal with him or her. You can also visualize ice crystals around your heart or genitals, if you need to.

When the day arrives that you come across the poppet in the freezer and can't remember for a moment what it is or why it's there, it's safe to assume that you are over that person and can now dispose of the poppet.

Note: If you are so obsessed with someone that you have begun stalking that person, or have become violent, you need to get professional psychological help as well as casting this spell.

⚮ Cooling Anger ⚮

Do you have a terrible temper? Does your hotheadedness create problems for you? Has anyone suggested that you get anger management training? Do you smash things, have a vicious tongue, or cause harm in some other way? Do you need to learn to control your temper for your own good as well as for the good of others? If so, the spell given above is easily adapted to help you. You will need:

+ a poppet of yourself (This could be anything from a sewn "voodoo doll" to a chess piece. Anything that represents you, in your mind, will do nicely.)
+ a pen or marker that will write on the poppet
+ a cup of sweetened mint tea

+ a sealable plastic bag that is big enough to hold the poppet
+ your freezer

Preparation

Get into a magickal mood, and create sacred space around the area where you will be working. The planet Mars rules anger, so inscribe the poppet with its symbol: ♂. Make a cup of mint tea, and add sugar, honey, or another sweetener to it. Drink half of the tea, then put the rest of it into the refrigerator. Leave it there until it has grown very cold.

Focus on your anger while you wait for the tea to cool. Think about all of the problems that it has caused for you and for others. Own that anger, and accept responsibility for it. Know that you are the only one who can do anything about it. Visualize all the positive changes that will likely be made in your life, and the lives of others, once you get your temper under control.

The Spell

Take the tea out of the refrigerator once it is cold. Raise power. Hold the poppet in your projective hand, and command it to cool off. Tell it that this is the end of the road for your bad temper. Put the poppet into the bag, and pour the cold tea over it. Seal the bag, and put it into your freezer. Stick it out of the way in a place where it won't be seen every time the freezer is opened.

Visualize your anger cooling as the tea freezes. Tell yourself that you will now rule yourself, instead of allowing your temper to rule you. Ground the power that you raised.

Afterward

Summon the feeling of ice water into your veins whenever you feel yourself getting angry. If you do have a tantrum, or indulge yourself in any other display of anger, get the poppet out of the freezer, and hold it until you cool down.

Note: If you are so out of control that your anger has caused you to commit crimes, such as arson or domestic violence, you need to get professional psychological help as well as casting this spell. If you care about your karma, you also need to accept justice or make restitution for these crimes.

◦ Tragedy Potion ◦

This potion is an emergency measure to use when tragedy strikes. I created it on 9/11/2001, after I watched the Twin Towers collapse on live television. It was surreal. I felt cold, numb, and horror-struck. I couldn't get my mind to truly grasp what had just happened and realized that I was in shock. I had a lot of calls to make to check on people, so I knew that I needed to quickly get myself grounded, centered, and balanced enough to do that. This potion worked. I hope that you will never need it, but here are the ingredients:

- ✦ hot chocolate (I used skim milk and a powder mix that contained high-quality cocoa. I have thankfully never had to make this potion again, so I don't know if instant hot chocolate would be as effective. Sugar is helpful in treating shock, so don't use a sugar-free chocolate mix unless you're diabetic.)
- ✦ essential oil of peppermint

The Potion

Get out a saucepan, a mug or cup, milk, a cocoa mix, a spoon, and oil of peppermint. Make the hot chocolate. Put your body on auto-pilot if need be, but keep enough awareness to do this carefully. If you do not pay attention, you may accidentally burn yourself, scald the milk, or set something on fire. As you stir the cocoa say repeatedly,

Isis, help me.

Pour the hot chocolate into a cup. Add one or two drops of essential oil of peppermint, and stir the cup just once. Some of the oil should be floating on the surface of the hot chocolate. Take a big gulp as soon as the chocolate is cool enough to drink. The peppermint will hit your system like a bolt of lightning and help to jolt you out of shock. Sip the rest of the potion slowly. You should be feeling much better by the time you finish the cup of hot chocolate. Have a second cup later, if you need to.

Note: This potion isn't for you if you are lactose-intolerant, allergic to chocolate or peppermint, or have any medical reason that precludes its use.

⁓ Demeter Spell for a Missing Child ⁓

We know from statistics that by the time we hear about a missing child, it is probably already too late to help her or him. All that is decent, hopeful, and compassionate in us responds to the terrible news, nonetheless, so why not cast a spell? We don't generally use magick for people without a specific request for magickal assistance, but if tearful parents are on television pleading for help from anyone who can give it, I think that we can take that request to include us as well.

Because her daughter Persephone was abducted by Hades, Demeter is a goddess who knows the unimaginable pain of losing a child and the fierce joy of getting that beloved child back. She is a powerful deity to turn to for help when a child disappears, no matter if the child is thought to be lost, to have run away, or to have been taken.

This is an urgent working, so the spell is best cast as soon as you learn that a child is missing. You will need:

+ a white candle
+ a white cloth (This needn't be anything large or fancy. A damask tablecloth is great, but a white towel or napkin will do.)

+ a picture of the missing child, a news article about the disappearance, or the child's name written on a piece of white paper

+ a pentacle or pentagram (Any type will do, even the symbol ⊗ drawn on a piece of paper.)

+ a handful of any type of grain (Barley is best, but rice, oatmeal, cornmeal, flour, or whatever you happen to have in your kitchen will do.)

+ *Optional*: some mullein (*Verbascum thapsiforme*)

+ *Optional*: all-black or all-white clothing

Preparation

Change your clothes if you are dressing for the spell. Gather the spell ingredients.

The Spell

Get into a magickal mood, and create sacred space around the area where you will be working. Put the white cloth on your altar or other working surface, and place the pentacle on it. Put the child's picture in the center of the pentacle, and place the candle upright on top of that. Working deosil, spread the grain around the pentacle's circle. Do the same with the mullein, if you're using that.

Raise power, and light the candle. Focus on the missing child. Concentrate on drawing that child back to safety or on leading searchers to her or him. If it appears that someone has taken the child, try to send that person the thought that it would be better to leave the child in a safe place, rather than to continue with the abduction. Channel as much energy into this as you possibly can.

Raise your hands over the candle. Focus on the child and the distraught family as you say:

Barley Mother, Giver of All,
Hear their pleas, answer my call.
By the power resident in grain,
Ease their sorrow, end their pain.
August Demeter, you are the key.
Rescue _____ as you did Peresphone.

Remain with the candle. Keep repeating the spell, or speak to
Demeter in your own words. Concentrate on the child while you
do this, focusing your attention on drawing her or him to safety.
When the candle burns out, ground the power that you raised,
and clean up. Take the grain (and mullein if you used it), and
scatter it outdoors.

Afterward

If you hear the wonderful news that the child has come home,
give thanks to Demeter by pouring out a libation of water to her.
Pour it first to the East and then to the West.

⚬ Crossroads Uncrossing Spell ⚬

One woe doth tread upon another's heel,
So fast they follow.
—William Shakespeare, *Hamlet*

Have you been having a hard time? Are things not going your
way lately? Do you seem to be thwarted at every turn? Does
everything in your life seem to be going wrong all at once?
Witches call such negative cycles "crossed conditions." These
cycles tend to pass on their own in time, but it's natural to want
to speed them on their way. Spells such as this one can help
to reverse a negative trend and restore positive conditions to
your life.

This spell can be cast at any time, but it is most powerful
on a Wednesday while the Moon is waning (the period between
Full Moon and New Moon—use a calendar to time it). You
will need:

+ a large purple candle with a flat bottom

+ a small black candle

+ a piece of thread or ribbon that is long enough to tie nine times around the purple candle

+ a capful of ammonia, lemon-scented, if possible

+ a handful of sea salt (Ordinary salt may be substituted.)

+ some black pepper

+ a dish or tray

+ a piece of black cloth that is large enough to wrap the purple candle in

Preparation

Identify nine aspects of your crossed condition. This might include problems such as communication failures, bad luck, bad timing, accidents, breakdowns, interruptions, ill health, wasted time, lost items, and so on. Be thorough. If you cannot identify nine aspects, things might not be as bad as you thought, and you may not need a spell. If you have more than nine aspects, group them together so that they total nine. If you think you will have trouble remembering all nine, make a list of them.

Next, identify a crossroad in your area. This must be a true crossroad, where two thoroughfares intersect to form a ✚ or an ✕ or one where three or more roads come together. If you have more than one crossroad available to you, choose the busiest one. You're going to be leaving the debris from your spell there, so consider traffic regulations and local laws about littering when you plan this part of the spell.

The Spell

Gather the spell materials. Get into a magickal mood, and create sacred space around the area where you will be working. Tie the thread or ribbon around the purple candle nine times near its base. Make a knot each time that you tie the thread, and name one of the aspects of your crossed condition as you tie the knot. (If you run out of thread or ribbon, get another piece and keep going.)

Light the black candle. Let it burn for a bit, then begin to drip its wax onto the purple candle. Drip it so that the wax forms crisscross patterns on the big candle to symbolize your crossed condition. Be sure to drip wax over the knots to seal them. When you're done, extinguish the black candle, and put it aside.

Place the tray or dish on your altar or other working surface. Set the purple candle upright in the middle, then pour the ammonia into the tray around its base. Working widdershins, sprinkle first the sea salt and then the black pepper around the candle. Use enough salt to absorb all of the ammonia.

Raise power, then light the purple candle. Hold your arms up and say:

> *By the power of the number nine,*
> *A positive cycle will be mine!*
> *Fulmination, culmination,*
> *An end to thee __(crossed aspect #1)__ !*
> *Fulmination, culmination,*
> *An end to thee __(crossed aspect #2)__ !*
> *Fulmination, culmination,*
> *An end to thee __(crossed aspect #3)__ !*

Continue this way until you have named all nine aspects of your crossed condition. Repeat this entire spell nine times while the candle burns. (Do not allow the candle to burn down too close to the ammonia-soaked salt, though, or you may get more fulmination than you bargained for.) After nine repetitions, say triumphantly:

> *Hard times are done*
> *And good times begun.*
> *By the power of the number nine,*
> *A more positive cycle is mine!*

Blow out the candle, to blow your crossed conditions away, and ground the power that you raised. Make sure that the candle is completely extinguished, then put all of the used spell materials onto the black cloth. Wrap it tightly around them, and take the bundle immediately to the crossroads.

Toss the bundle over your left shoulder, preferably in a spot where it will be repeatedly run over. Leave the bundle there, and do not look back at it. If it is easiest to toss it from a car, that's fine.

Your crossed conditions will begin to lift within nine days.

⚘ Hex-Breaker Spell ⚘

Do you suspect that someone may be working magickally against you? Do you fear that you have been cursed? Chances are that you're mistaken and simply experiencing the normal vicissitudes of life, but casting a spell can relieve your fears.

This spell will remove anything negative that has been cast on you or against you. It will do no harm if you're wrong and there is no hex or curse. It can be cast at any time, anywhere. You will need:

- ✦ a chain (Any type of light metal chain that can be broken with a stick will do, but choose one whose size represents the size of the hex that you suspect you may be under.)

- ✦ a bamboo rod (This must be bamboo and of sufficient size and strength to break the chain that you have selected. If you cannot obtain a large enough stick, use several smaller bamboo rods, and replace them as they break or wear out. Can't find a bamboo stick? Try shops that sell Asian goods. Paper window shades, for example, are often wrapped around a bamboo rod for weight.)

- ✦ a white candle

Preparation

You're going to really whomp that chain, so choose a place where you can do this safely and without interruption.

The Spell

Gather the spell materials. Get into a magickal mood, and create sacred space around the area where you will be working. Light the candle.

Hold the chain in both hands, and raise power. Focus on the reasons why you think that you have been hexed. Concentrate on the energy signature of the hex as you perceive it. Use your mind to channel that energy into the chain and trap it in the links. Use whatever visualization you find helpful, such as picturing dark light streaming out of you and winding itself around and through the links, then solidifying to become one with the chain.

This is a crucial part of the spell, transferring the hex or curse from you into the chain, so take your time with it. The transfer is complete when you perceive a difference in the chain, such as feeling it grow heavier or become warm. If strenuous magickal effort creates no perceptible difference in the chain, it is likely that there is no hex or curse on you. In that case, ground power immediately and discard all the spell materials. If you succeed in transferring a hex or curse into the chain, continue with the spell.

Hold the chain triumphantly aloft with both hands, in a victory stance. Face each direction in turn, beginning with the North, and say:

Guardians of the North, grant me power!
Guardians of the West, send me strength!
Guardians of the South, give me energy!
Guardians of the East, know my spirit!

Throw the chain down, and smash it with the bamboo stick until it breaks. If you are angry about having been hexed, use this process to vent that anger. You may find the work easier if you stretch the chain taut and secure its ends or drape it over something, such as a rock or cinder block. Use whatever is available to you, but only use things you cannot harm.

As you strike the chain, imagine that you are striking the hex or curse that has been placed upon you. Visualize it weakening as the chain weakens and permanently broken when the chain breaks. Try to break the chain before the candle burns out. When it breaks, say triumphantly:

> *Spell completed,*
> *Curse defeated!*

Ground the power that you raised, and clean up. You should feel lighter and proud of yourself for having overcome the hex. Throw the chain away, or keep it as an amulet against future attempts to hex you.

If you are tempted to cast something negative on whoever you think sent the hex, don't give in to that temptation. Two very good reasons for this are, first, that you could be wrong about who hexed you, and, second, that this type of magick will only hurt you. Black magick does more harm to the one who casts it than to the one it is cast upon, so you don't need to take action in order for the one who hexed you to receive payback for it.

⁖ Lady of Bright Inspiration Spell ⁖

Are you out of ideas? Could your creativity use a boost? This spell creates a magickally charged candle that you can burn whenever you need inspiration. It can be cast at any time but is most powerfully cast five nights before the Full Moon (use a calendar to time this). You will need:

+ an amethyst
+ a large purple candle with a flat bottom, such as a pillar candle (A round candle is best, but any shape will work. Any shade of purple is fine.)
+ a cauldron that is large enough to hold the candle (A bowl, pot, dish, or other container can be substituted if you first hold your hands over it and say, "You are now my cauldron." Be sure that the candle will sit stably in the bottom of the cauldron and be unlikely to topple over.)
+ one-quarter cup canola oil (This must be canola oil, because Canola is an Irish goddess of inspiration. You can get it from a grocery store.)
+ three drops of blue food coloring
+ two drops of red food coloring (Five drops of violet or purple food coloring can be used instead of the red and blue.)

Preparation

Assemble all of the spell ingredients, preferably in sacred space. Face East. Pour the oil into the cauldron, and add the food coloring. Use the index finger of your projective hand to stir the oil deosil until it is thoroughly mixed to a uniform purple color. Be sure to stir it deosil, because you are working an attraction spell to draw the energies of inspiration to you.

Put the amethyst in the center of the cauldron, and leave it there overnight. Place the cauldron near a window that faces East, if possible.

The Spell

Get into a magickal mood the next day, and create sacred space around the area where you will be working. You can do this at any time of day, but it is most powerfully done in moonlight. Raise power. Focus on inspiration as you face East, and dress the candle to charge it with power. Hold the candle with your receptive hand. Dip the index finger of your projective hand into the oil in the cauldron, and rub the candle with it from bottom to top. Repeat this until the entire candle is covered, saying:

> Cerridwen, White Lady of Inspiration,
> Bless this cauldron with the waters of inspiration.
> Brigid, Lady of Bright Inspiration,
> Bless this candle with the fires of inspiration.
> Nimuë, White Lady of Day,
> Enchant this spell with inspiration.

There is likely to still be some oil in the cauldron when you finish dressing the candle. Push the amethyst to the side of the cauldron. Hold the candle by its wick, and set it upright in the middle of the cauldron, so that any remaining oil puddles around its base. Thank the goddesses, and ground the power that you raised.

Leave the cauldron, oil, and candle as they are, and put them in a safe place until you need them. It isn't a problem if the oil should dry up. If your need for inspiration is constant, wash off the amethyst, and keep it with you as a charm.

Afterward

Light the candle whenever you need inspiration or new ideas or want to get your creative juices flowing. You can burn the candle whenever you like, but it will work most powerfully in moonlight. Each time that you light it, say:

> Flame of Inspiration, guide me.

Burn the candle for as long as you need, and then extinguish it. Never blow it out, because you might accidentally extinguish the magick. Use a candle snuffer instead, or wet your fingers and pinch the wick to put the candle out.

Depending on what type of candle you use, its wax may melt down into the cauldron. It's fine if this happens. Leave the wax there until the candle has been consumed, the magick is exhausted, and you are ready to clean out the cauldron. If you use a pillar candle, its wax may need to be poured off or trimmed away after each use, in order to keep the wick exposed. If you must trim the candle, put the excess wax back into the cauldron.

Discard the candle when it is finished. The cauldron and amethyst can be washed and used again, to repeat this spell or for another magickal purpose.

⁓ Scene of the Crime Spell ⁓

Hecate (pronounced "heh-ka-tay") is a powerful goddess whose dominion includes crime scenes, so she is present in places where crimes have been committed. When a crime is particularly unjust or gruesome, or remains unsolved, her presence may linger in that place for many years.

This spell can be cast at the scene of any crime whose perpetrator has not yet been caught. It should be cast at night, because Hecate also has dominion over darkness. The spell can be cast on any night, but it is best cast on a Saturday. It is worded for a male criminal, but you can alter the wording if a female or a group of perpetrators is suspected.

Note: It is said that Hecate is likely to give you what you need—not necessarily what you ask for. For example, you could want the criminal convicted and imprisoned, but she could think it better to have him die in a shootout with the police. The reverse is also possible. You might be thinking about prison brutality or the death penalty when you cast the spell, but she might decide that it is better for your karma to have him evade the justice system and pay for his crime in some other way. You may never learn what outcome your spell had, but you can be sure that Hecate is working to help you. She is a very active goddess in the modern world, and invoking her may form a permanent connection between you. Be aware of these things before you decide to use this spell. If you decide to proceed, this is what you will need:

+ three black candles

+ three sticks of incense, preferably patchouli

+ black pepper

+ a sharp lead pencil

+ a picture or other image of a black spider (If you draw this yourself, use the lead pencil.)

+ black yarn or ribbon, cut into long pieces (The more serious the crime, or the farther away the criminal is suspected to be, the longer the pieces should be.)

+ one bottle of apple cider vinegar (Any type of vinegar may be substituted, but that is the most powerful kind to use for this spell.)

+ *Optional*: anything that the criminal touched or left behind

+ *Optional*: three eggs and three onions that have been left overnight at the crime scene to absorb its energy

Preparation

Use the pencil to carve the words "the criminal" into each of the candles. Write it on them instead, if the pencil will not penetrate the wax. It's fine if the words are difficult to make out on the candle.

Use the pieces of black yarn or ribbon to construct an image that represents a spider's web. It needn't be accurate or artistic, just something that seems like a spider web to you.

The Spell

Gather all of the spell ingredients, except the pencil, and bring them to the crime scene. Get into a magickal mood. Arrange the spider web on the ground, as close as possible to the spot where the crime is thought to have taken place. Position the candles upright in a triangle at the center of the web. If you have something that the criminal touched, place this in the middle of the triangle of candles—or near the web, if it is a large item. Arrange the incense near the candles, and place the spider on the web.

Raise power. Work widdershins to pour out the black pepper so that it makes a circle around the web. As you do this, visualize snaring the criminal in your web and bringing him to justice. Light the candles and the incense. Watch them burn for a bit, as you meditate on what happened at the scene. Focus on justice catching up with the criminal, and say:

> *Great Mother Hecate,*
> *Hear me, hear me, hear me,*
> *In this place that was defiled*
> *By the one who is reviled.*
> *Seek him, find him,*
> *Catch him, bind him!*

> *Dark Mother Hecate,*
> *Hear me, hear me, hear me.*
> *Let the one sought*
> *By justice be caught.*
> *Hold him fast*
> *In bonds that last.*

> *Great Mother Hecate,*
> *Seek him, find him,*
> *Catch him, bind him!*
> *So mote it be!*

The candles and the incense will still be burning after you cast the spell. While they burn, take the vinegar and begin pouring or sprinkling it in every part of the crime scene that feels as though it needs to be purified. Visualize the criminal being caught. Imagine him in handcuffs, or sitting in the back of a police car, or on trial, or behind bars, or wearing an orange jumpsuit, or whatever image works for you. Pour as much energy as you can into that image. Repeat the spell, if that feels necessary to you.

Ground the power that you raised, once the candles and the incense have burned down. If possible, leave everything at the crime scene overnight, and clean up the area the next morning. If the crime scene felt heavy with negative energy before you cast the spell, you should find that it feels lighter when you return to it.

Afterward

The gods have their own sense of time, so be patient while you wait expectantly for this spell to manifest. Be mindful that justice can take other forms besides those that the criminal justice system metes out.

Optional: To thank Hecate for hearing your request, offer her the eggs and onions that were left overnight at the crime scene. Do this by taking them to a crossroads where three roads meet and leaving them beside the road for her on the night of a Full Moon.

Do not take these offerings home or keep them in your car, because that may forge an unwanted link between you and the criminal. Leave them outdoors, preferably at or near the crime scene, until you take them to the crossroads. It's fine if someone takes them or if animals eat them before the Full Moon.

⋰ Boundary Spell ⋱

Coexisting with other human beings can be stressful, especially in crowded conditions such as cities and large households. When we have trouble getting along with people, it is often because they overstep the boundaries that we have unconsciously set, then failed to communicate.

The best approach is to deal directly and honestly with others, to tell them frankly but kindly what we expect or will not tolerate. But if you've already tried that and it hasn't worked, this spell can help you to define and defend your boundaries. It invokes Zemlya, a Slavic mother goddess.

The spell can be cast at any time, but it is most powerful on a Saturday or when the Sun or Moon is in Saturn (use an astrological almanac to determine this). Use caution, as always, when working with fire. You will need:

+ two pieces of paper
+ a pen or marker with black ink
+ some dirt or potting soil
+ a black candle
+ a fireproof container
+ water for fire safety
+ a digging tool, such as a trowel or large spoon

Preparation

Identify the groups and individuals who regularly overstep your bounds. Is there someone who habitually calls or visits you at inconvenient times? Do you have noisy neighbors, meddlesome relatives, inconsiderate friends, or a job that eats away at your personal life? Consider all of the recurring invasions of your privacy, time, personal space, or property, and write them down.

Be reasonable about this. It may annoy you whenever someone parks in front of your house, but if this is on a public street, you have no right to claim that space as your personal property or to defend it magickally as such. But if someone habitually uses that public parking space as a private mechanic shop or car wash and drives you nuts with annoying noise, mess, or behavior, and if the police cannot or will not help you with this, that is another matter.

When you finish your list, put it away for at least twenty-four hours. Take it out a day or two later, and reread it. Close your eyes, and meditate on what you have written. Review it again after you meditate. Consider whether or not you have taken all possible nonmagickal actions to deal with these things, such as writing letters or making phone calls. Determine whether your list is complete, whether there are items that don't belong on it, and whether there are actions you should take before proceeding with the spell. Make changes and take action, as needed.

Next, define your boundaries, and write them down on another sheet of paper. Include the things that you will no longer allow, such as "phone calls after 11 pm," "smoking in my home," "dogs on my lawn," or whatever the case may be. Also list the things that you will no longer do, such as "work weekends," "lend my car," "cover for others," or whatever your issues may be.

This is your Action Plan, so beside each item list the things you plan to do about it. For example, if smoking in your home is a problem, you might write next to that item "Remove all ashtrays from the house. Let guests know that they must go out on the balcony to smoke." If people walking on your lawn is a problem, you might write "Put up Keep Off the Grass signs. Plant a hedge." or "Install a fence."

Put the Action Plan away for at least twenty-four hours. Take it out and reread it after some time has passed. Close your eyes, and meditate on what you have written. Review the Action Plan again after you meditate. Consider the wisdom of these actions and their feasibility. Will you actually do these things? Remind yourself that this spell won't work unless you carry out your Action Plan. If you would like to add things, change things, or remove things from the paper, do it.

The Spell

Assemble the spell materials, and get into a magickal mood. Create sacred space around the area where you will be working. Put your Action Plan on your altar or other working surface, and place a small pile of earth in its middle. Spread the soil out until it lines the four sides of the paper. Place the black candle upright in the now empty center of the paper.

Position the fireproof container on a surface that will not scorch if its bottom gets hot. Take the first paper you prepared, and put it beside the container. Place the water nearby.

Take some of the soil from the sides of the paper, and carefully push or sprinkle it near the candle each time you say Zemlya's name. When the spell is complete, all of the soil should be around the base of the candle.

Raise power, light the candle, and cast the spell. Hold your hands with their palms upward on either side of the candle, and say:

> Beloved Zemlya, Mother Earth,
> Protect me from annoyance, interference, and incursion,
> From harassment, intrusion, and invasion.
> Beloved Zemlya, Mother Earth,
> Protect me from all that besieges, poaches, or encroaches,
> From all that seeps or creeps or prevents sleep.
> Mati Syra Zemlya, Moist Mother Earth,
> Protect me from all that presses, stresses,
> depresses, or trespasses,
> From all that disrupts, interrupts, pushes,
> assails, or infringes.
> Beloved Zemlya, Mother Earth,
> Protect me from all that is rude, crude, or intrudes,
> From all that crowds or is too loud.
> Mati Syra Zemlya, Moist Mother Earth,
> Protect me from everyone and everything
> That would overstep my boundaries!

Carefully move the candle aside. Pick up the Action Plan by either end, and tip all of the soil into the fireproof container. Replace the candle in the center of the Action Plan. Take the other paper from its place next to the fireproof container. Touch one end of it to the candle flame, set it ablaze, and carefully drop it into the container. The paper should burn until it is completely consumed, and then extinguish itself. (Relight it from the candle or douse it with water, if necessary.)

Concentrate on ending all violations of your boundaries as you watch the paper burn. Visualize your boundaries in terms of time (your private life and personal time) and space (your home, possessions, and personal space). Mentally place glowing light around all that you would have this spell henceforth hold inviolate.

Hold that image until the paper is consumed and the candle burns itself out, then pour the water into the container with the ashes and the soil. Take the container, your Action Plan, and the digging tool outside (or to a potted plant, if you must work indoors). Dig a hole, and bury the Action Plan. Pour the mud and ashes over it, then cover the hole. Place your hands over it, touching the earth, then ground the power that you raised.

Remember the spot where you buried the spell debris. Mark it in some way, such as with stones or twigs, if you are concerned about forgetting its exact location. Even better, plant something on top of it.

Go back inside, and clean up. Discard the candle and whatever remains of the incense. Wash everything else.

Afterward

Be vigilant in patrolling the borders you have defined for yourself. The best way to keep this spell working is to carry out all the items on your Action Plan. If you need some magickal help with this, water the place where you buried the spell debris whenever you have problems with boundary issues. Take a tiny pinch of dirt from that spot, sprinkle it on your head, and ask Mati Syra Zemlya for her help.

∴ Untwisting Spell ∴

This spell helps to straighten out someone who is all screwed up. You can cast it for yourself or for someone who has asked you for magickal help. Be sure to have permission before casting this spell for anyone, and remember that magick is not a substitute for therapy, medical care, or ending a violent relationship.

This spell can be cast at any time, but it is most powerful when cast on the night of a Full Moon (use a calendar to time it). You will need:

✦ an onion

✦ a sharp kitchen knife

✦ a spiral candle, preferably a taper (You will be naming this candle for the person to be untwisted, so choose whatever color candle seems appropriate to you for this person—or use a white candle. You can find spiral tapers in housewares shops.)

✦ an essential oil or other concentrated liquid form of an herb or flower, such as pure vanilla extract (The oil, or whatever you are substituting for it, should also be appropriate to the person for whom the spell is to be cast, such as a plant that you associate with the person or with his or her problem.)

✦ a dishcloth or paper towel

Preparation

Dress the candle at least one day before you cast the spell. Assemble the candle, the oil, and the knife in a place where you can work calmly and without interruption. Create sacred space around the area.

Turn the candle wick-down over a cloth or paper towel. Cut away the wax at the bottom of the candle, until the wick is exposed on that side. Focus on the person to be untwisted. Hold the inverted candle and say:

> *I name this candle for _____.*

You must believe that this candle now represents that person, or the spell will not work properly.

Open the bottle of oil, or whatever you are substituting for it. Use your receptive hand to hold the bottom of the candle and slowly turn it widdershins as you drip the oil onto it with your projective hand. Allow the oil to spiral downward, following the grooves in the candle from the bottom to its tip. As you do this, concentrate on the person and exactly how and why you think that he or she is "screwed up." The candle will drip, so be sure to have a cloth or paper towel beneath it.

Leave the candle in a safe place, such as on your altar, to dry overnight. It should have flecks of dried oil all over it the next day. Put the candle in a holder, upside down. You can cast the spell immediately, or leave the dressed candle on your altar until you are ready for the spell.

The Spell

Put the candle, knife, and onion on your altar or other working surface. Get into a magickal mood, and create sacred space around the area. Focus on the person who needs to be untwisted. Hold the onion while you do this, and visualize it as that person. You must believe that the onion now represents her or him. Raise power and say:

> *Onion, I name you _____.*
> *As I cut away this skin,*
> *I make you ready for transformation.*
> *I remove your resistance to it.*

Raise power. Cut the skin from the onion, then light the candle.

Begin to cut into the onion, carefully peeling away layer after layer until you come to the bulb at its center. Take your time, and concentrate on the person while you do this, naming your purpose aloud as you go. Say whatever feels appropriate, such as "I cut away your negativity," or "I remove those who have negative influence over you." If you find any diseased spots in the onion, think of it as psychic surgery as you carefully excise them. Keep going until you reach the bulb at the center of the onion. Visualize it as the core of the person.

Some onions have a double bulb, with a smaller bulb attached to the main one. One way to interpret this, if you encounter a double bulb while casting this spell, is to see the smaller bulb as representing someone (such as an energy vampire—a person who sucks the life energy out of others) or something (such as an addiction or a bad habit) negative that has become attached to the person for whom the spell is being cast. Remove the small bulb if you find one by very carefully cutting it away without damaging the main bulb.

Throw away all the cut-off parts of the onion, wash your hands and the knife, and clean the surface where you worked. The candle should still be burning, with the onion bulb in front of it. Focus on the candle. Make it the person whom you are trying to help. Imagine that the candle untwists the person as it burns. Raise the power higher, and command,

> *Do not resist me as I untwist thee,*
> *do not resist me as I untwist thee.*

Repeat this as many times as feel necessary, while you watch the candle burn down completely. Hold your hands near the candle, close but not touching it, if this will help you to concentrate. Focus on exactly what you mean by untwisting.

We can be wrong about what we think will help other people, and even wrong about what will help ourselves. To avoid imposing your will on the person or trying to manifest a result that is not needed, ask the Goddess to untwist the person in whatever way would be best. Ground the power that you raised.

The onion peelings represent all that was wrong with him or her, so get them out of your house immediately after the candle finishes burning. Once you have done that, set the onion bulb on a windowsill or in some other place where the morning Sun will reach it. Tell it (the person) that he or she will be reborn with the Sun in the morning and that everything is going to be all right.

The last time that I cast this spell, I put the onion bulb on a small glass dish and made a circle of clear quartz crystals and dried red roses around it. I did that because it felt right to me for the person and for the working. I left it overnight atop my pentacle, on a windowsill. You can arrange whatever feels right to you for the onion, or simply leave it there alone.

Plant the onion bulb the next day. Do this indoors if the earth is too cold to plant it outside. This act will serve to ground the power you raised. If the onion happens to take root and bloom, that is a wonderful sign that the spell has worked.

Afterward

This spell should work within a few days, even if the onion simply withers in the ground. The person for whom it is cast may experience a sudden and dramatic change for the better, or he or she may begin to gradually improve.

Variation

Two or more witches, each working alone at home, can cast this spell at the same time for the same person.

⁙ White Goddess Nightmare Spell ⁙

Everyone has the occasional nightmare, but you can use this spell if you are afflicted with bad dreams. Nightmares can be stubborn, so the spell takes three days to complete. It can be cast at any time but is best begun one week after the Full Moon (use a calendar to time it). You will need:

+ a besom (A brand-new broom can be substituted.)

+ a white candle

+ several sprigs of fresh rosemary or a handful of dried rosemary (Anise or aniseed could be substituted.)

+ a pentacle (A fancy one is great, but the ✪ symbol drawn on a piece of paper will do.)

+ white ribbon

+ enough chamomile to make three cups of tea

+ *Optional*: rosemary incense (Cedar could be substituted.)

DAY ONE

Preparation

Get out your besom, and tie a white ribbon around the handle, where it joins the bristles. Hold the broom in both hands. Face each direction in turn, beginning with North, and say, "I dedicate this broom to the White Goddess." Place the broom near or behind the door to your bedroom (or wherever you usually sleep) in a place where it can remain undisturbed for three days.

If you are using incense, open a window, and burn it in your bedroom. Take the besom, and hold it over the smoke for a while to smudge it, then return it to its place by the door. If you are not using incense, proceed to this next part of the spell.

Assemble the candle, the rosemary, and the pentacle on your altar or other working surface. Get into a magickal mood, and create sacred space. Put the pentacle on the altar, and place the white candle in its center. Work widdershins to arrange the rosemary in a circle around the candle.

The Spell

Raise power and light the candle. While it burns, say:

> *Khmara shall not torture me,*
> *And I shall not torture myself.*
> *By the White Goddess, I banish my nightmares.*
> *In sleep, let me not find them;*
> *By day, let me not mind them;*
> *Finally, let Niorun bind them.*
> *Khmara shall not torture me,*
> *And I shall not torture myself.*
> *By the White Goddess,*
> *My nightmares are banished.*
> *So mote it be!*

When the candle has burned down, ground the power that you raised. Make certain that the candle is completely extinguished, then put its remains anywhere in your bedroom. Place the pentacle under your bed (or beneath your mattress), with its top point facing the foot of the bed. You are working a banishing, so it is important for the pentacle to be placed that way.

If you have used fresh rosemary, tie the sprigs into a bunch with some white ribbon, and hang it over your bed. If you have used dried rosemary, divide it into five roughly equal piles. Place one pile in each of the four corners of your bedroom, and place the fifth pile under your bed, atop the pentacle. Ground the power that you raised.

Make yourself a cup of chamomile tea at bedtime. If you have a white mug or teacup, use that. Say the words of the spell aloud between sips of the tea, then go to bed.

DAY TWO and DAY THREE

The Spell

You should feel good when you wake up. If you had a disturbing dream, it should have been less intense than usual.

Open a window. Take the besom, and sweep your entire room, sweeping toward the doorway. This is psychic sweeping, so the bristles needn't touch the floor. As you work, visualize the room being cleared of all negative energy. Chant this sweeping spell as you work:

> Besom, besom, White Goddess broom,
> Sweep all nightmares from this room.

When you finish, stand in the doorway. Regard the room and your bed. The atmosphere should feel lighter, and you should feel strong and positive.

Drink the tea and say the spell at bedtime. Each morning, sweep out your room while you chant the sweeping spell. You should be free of nightmares by the third night. The candle can then be discarded, and the pentacle thrown away or put back in its usual place. The besom is now sacred to the White Goddess, so keep it separate from your household tools, and reserve it exclusively for magickal use. Leave the rosemary in your bedroom for as long as possible.

Afterward

If the nightmares return within six months of casting this spell, you're dealing with something that you need to consult a doctor about. You stated that you would not harm yourself in the spell, so if the nightmares come back, it's your higher self directing you to seek medical care.

If you cannot find a doctor who can help you, seek treatment from a mental health practitioner. If you have been there and done that but still the nightmares persist, they may be caused by something that happened in a previous life—something important enough to come through to this incarnation. If you suspect that may be the case, seek out a reputable past-life therapist.

❦6❧

Magickal Candle Gardens

Witches receive a lot of requests for help. People who are ill, grieving, healing, lonely, victimized, challenged in some other way, or concerned for someone else often turn to us for assistance. It isn't possible to cast spells for everyone, so our usual practice is to light candles for people with the magickal intent of sending energy for whatever their specific need is.

Witches also work magickally on personal objectives. We often work on several of these simultaneously, such as health, prosperity, and protection. Creating magickal candle gardens is one way to keep these practices organized.

A candle garden is a collection of attractively arranged candles, usually of different sizes, that are all burned at the same time. When a candle garden is meant simply for home decoration, its candles are often all the same color, shape, and scent. They are generally purchased in the same place, at the same time, and chosen only for appearance.

It takes a great deal more thought and planning to create a magickal candle garden. Such a "garden" should contain separate candles for each person, condition, problem, idea, or issue for which its candles are burned. Each candle should be carefully selected so that its size, shape, color, or scent resonates with its magickal intent or with the person or thing that the candle is meant to represent. Each of the candles in a magickal garden should be unique, yet, as in a flower garden, all of the parts of the whole must work harmoniously together. The candle arrangement should please the eye, and the different scents should mingle pleasantly rather than clash with one another.

A magickal candle garden is personal. You determine how your garden will look, what its purpose will be, when it will be used, and how long you will burn the candles each time you activate the garden. You can burn them every day, on certain days of the week, at appointed phases of the Moon, whenever you have need, or simply whenever you feel like lighting them. The more frequently that a candle garden is used, the stronger its magick will grow.

⁓ Making a Magickal Candle Garden ⁓

You will need:

+ candles for each magickal goal, in appropriate sizes, shapes, scents, and colors (Use large candles for long-term goals that you will be working toward for some time, and smaller candles for short-term objectives.)

+ a tray, mirror, dish, bowl, tile, or other fire-safe container or surface in or on which to construct the garden

+ an altar candle, preferably a simple white taper

+ *Optional*: herbs, charms, crystals, images, or other items that you feel enhance the magick or appearance of your garden

+ *Optional*: oil for dressing the candles

+ *Optional*: incense, to burn when you light the candles

Charging the Candles

Once you have selected the candles for your garden, you must charge them. Consider your garden's purpose. Is it meant to encourage or to halt? What kind of energy is it meant to send? The magick of your garden will be strongest if the energy of all the candles is flowing in like manner. Assess your purpose in charging each candle, and word the charge accordingly. For example, it might be better to charge a candle to support your efforts to find a job, rather than charging it to end your financial problems; or to charge a candle to help end someone's loneliness, rather than to help them find love.

Once you have determined the wording, charge the candles. There are many ways to do this, but here is a simple one. Assemble all the components for your garden. Get into a magickal mood, and create sacred space around the area where you will be working. Place the altar candle in the empty garden, light it, and raise power.

Take the first garden candle, and hold it in both hands. Focus for a moment on that candle's purpose, then name it aloud. Concentrate on transferring magickal energy from your hands to the candle. (If you are using oil, rub the candle with it while you do this.) Hold the candle by its wick, place it upright in the garden, and say,

> *This candle will glow, and its magick will grow.*
> *This candle will glow, and its magick will flow.*

Continue this procedure until all of the candles have been charged and placed in the garden. Arrange them in whatever way seems most magickal and attractive to you. If you are incorporating charms, stones, statues, or other items with your garden, add them now.

When you like the way the garden looks, hold your hands over the candles. Concentrate on the garden's purpose and magickal objectives. Focus that intent into your hands, then transmit it to the candles. Say:

> *This garden is dedicated to the Lord and the Lady.*
> *It will create change, but never cause harm.*

When you feel that the candles are sufficiently charged, extinguish the altar candle. You can then ground the power that you raised, or you can activate the garden for the first time, and ground power afterwards.

Activating the Magick of a Candle Garden

When you want to release your garden's magick, get into a magickal mood, and focus on its intent. Create sacred space around it, and raise power. Light the altar candle, then use it to light the garden candles. As you light each one, name its purpose aloud.

Once all the candles are burning, stand back a bit and regard your garden. Visualize magickal energy shooting from each candle toward its goal. Focus on the changes your garden is meant to bring about, visualizing them as already accomplished. Raise your arms, and say in a strong, clear voice:

> *The magick is unpent and sent.*

Allow the candles to continue burning for as long as feels necessary to you, then extinguish them. (Many witches feel that to blow out a candle is to extinguish its magick or to undo the spell. If you feel this way, you should use a candle snuffer for your garden. Some witches believe that candles should always be extinguished in reverse order to that in which they were lit. If this resonates with you, do it.) Ground the power that you raised, and have something to drink.

The magickal potency of your garden will be increased if you make a small ritual of its activation. You can do this in whatever way you like, such as by wearing the same ritual clothes or mask each time, by playing the same music, burning the same incense, using the same ritual movements or hand gestures, and so on.

Maintaining the Garden

As with a real garden, you will need to tend this one on a regular basis. Instead of watering and pulling weeds, you'll need to trim candles, scrape up wax, and remove or replace candles as needed. You will remove a candle when its goal is reached and its work is done. You will replace a candle when it is spent, but its objective has not yet manifested. You will add a new candle whenever you want to incorporate an additional magickal objective into the garden.

Charge all new candles before you add them to the garden. If you consider this maintenance a sacred task, your garden's magick will flourish.

Different Types of Gardens

Various gardens can be created for different purposes. The following are a few examples of some of the many types of magickal candle gardens that you can create.

⸱ Garden of Ambition ⸱

In this garden you use a separate candle for each of your goals. A Garden of Ambition that is focused on work might, for example, include candles for a raise, a promotion, recognition, better assignments, and so on. If the garden also included personal goals, there might also be a candle for being more organized, one for getting into shape, one for keeping on budget, or whatever your individual goals might be.

Purple, silver, and dark green, for ambition, are appropriate candle colors for this garden; so are red for advancement and orange for success. Ogun is a god who helps with achieving goals. His colors of black, dark blue, light green, and red are also appropriate for the candles in this garden.

Appropriate charms for a Garden of Ambition include eight bay leaves or traditional offerings to Ogun, such as hot peppers, small bags of salt, and palm fronds. His customary altar furnishings of an iron cauldron and small metal objects, such as chains, wires, nails, and miniature tools, could also be incorporated in the garden.

Focus on moving forward when you activate this garden and on your action plan for reaching each goal. It would be unreasonable to only rely on magick, so also try to take a concrete step, however small it might be, toward each goal each day.

⋅ Garden of Compassion ⋅

In this garden you place a separate candle for each person who has asked you for magickal help. You use large candles for ongoing work, such as for someone with cancer or a heart condition, or for a child with special needs. You use smaller candles for people who are experiencing temporary challenges such as failed relationships, lost jobs, illnesses, or crossed conditions. Tea lights are good for single wish-me-luck lightings, for someone who has a court date, a job interview, or an exam, for example.

Candle colors for this garden can relate to each issue, such as white for protection or uncrossing, blue for hope or truth, green for healing or acceptance, brown for balance or grounding, pink for love or happiness, and so on. You might instead choose a candle because it reminds you, in some way, of the person for whom you charge it to work magick.

The garden might also contain charms of compassion such as a jade plant, a rose quartz heart, or an image of Kwan Yin, Lady of Compassion. Lotus and sandalwood incense are appropriate choices to burn with the candles.

When activating this garden, focus on sending energy to each person as you light his or her candle. To prevent depletion, make sure that when you raise power for this, you gather it from sunlight, storms, moonlight, trees, wind, or other natural sources instead of using your personal power.

◌ Garden of Thanksgiving ◌

Count your blessings, and notice that your cup is at least half full. What are you thankful for? In this garden you include a candle for each of your blessings. Each person's garden will be unique, but your blessings might include things such as good health, your family, your friends, your career, and the roof over your head. Items that relate to your blessings, such as pictures of friends or family members, are appropriate additions to this garden.

To whom will you be giving thanks? Images of a matron goddess or patron god are also appropriate for this garden, as are more general images such as those of the Lord and the Lady. You might instead incorporate images of gods and goddesses who have specific dominion over your blessings. (See "*Optional:* Invocation" on page 82 for ideas.) If you are giving thanks to the Universe rather than to deities, images of stars, planets, or constellations would be good charms for your garden.

You can double the magick of your Garden of Thanksgiving by focusing on maintaining your blessings, as well as on giving thanks for them, when you activate your garden.

◌ Morning Garden ◌

A Morning Garden should face East, where it greets the rising Sun each day. In it you place candles for things that you want to help grow, such as plans, projects, children, gardens, and businesses. You also include candles for things that are beginning, such as healing, artistic endeavors, enlightenment, new friendship, and new love, to encourage their growth and success. Yellow and rose-pink candles are appropriate for this garden. Good charms for it include bells, gongs, and conch shells.

Images of deities who have dominion over the dawn and auspicious beginnings, such as Aurora, Aya, Bast, Eos, Isis,

Janus, Ushas, or the Zorya, are also appropriate additions. This garden should be activated in the morning.

⌇ Evening Garden ⌇

An Evening Garden should face West, where it bids farewell to the Sun each night. In it you place candles for things that you want to end or go away, such as problems, hardships, illnesses, stresses, bad habits, negative patterns, toxic relationships, and so on. You also include candles for things that are ending, such as phases, relationships, situations, or life stages, to encourage their satisfactory completion.

Black, dark blue, dark plum, and dark gray are appropriate candle colors for this garden. Sprigs of rosemary and images of deities who have dominion over the sunset, such as Baal, the Hesperides, Janus, Nephthys, Sekhmet, and the Zorya, are also appropriate additions. This garden should be activated in the evenings.

⌇ Garden of the Wider World ⌇

Whatever the spiritual path, if one follows it correctly, there comes a time when one is more concerned for others than for oneself. In this garden you include candles for each global issue or problem that you care passionately about. Your candles might, for example, represent the ozone layer, the Amazon rain forest, hunger, terrorism, overpopulation, coral reefs, land mines, an endangered species, AIDS, or whatever you worry about. Such things require long-term solutions, so you use large candles for this garden.

Alternately or additionally, your garden might contain a candle for each place you care deeply about. This might be a continent, a country, a mountain, a river, your neighborhood, your ancestral homeland, or wherever your heart lies. The garden might also contain candles for groups of people you are concerned about, such as children, refugees, earthquake victims, and so on. There might also be candles to represent organizations whose international work you appreciate and would like to see flourish. These might be Greenpeace, UNICEF, PETA, the Red Cross or Red Crescent, Amnesty International, Doctors Without Borders, or whatever groups represent your interests.

Plan on giving this garden room to grow, because you are likely to find yourself frequently adding candles to it after you watch the news or read newspapers. When activating a Garden of the Wider World, focus on sending positive energy to each problem or group as you light its candle. Dragon's blood is an appropriate incense to burn when you activate the candles.

It will be a time of great happiness whenever you discover that one of this garden's candles is no longer needed.

·:·7·:·

Tea Potions

The brewing of magickal potions is a traditional skill of witches. Images of the cackling witches in *Macbeth* might come to mind, with their bubbling cauldron and horrible potion ingredients, or one may think of Cerridwen, whose legendary potion had to brew for a year in order to yield three drops of magickal elixir—but in reality, potions can be made quickly, simply, and from ordinary ingredients.

Tea is inherently magickal because it incorporates all four elements: boiling water (Fire and Water), herbs (Earth), and aromatic steam (Air). To make any cup of tea with magickal intent is to brew a potion. To drink a potion is to cast an indrinking spell, as you draw the magickal power of the brew into yourself.

The potions given here are simple spells that can be cast at any time. They are best made in privacy when you are calm, centered, and feeling able to enchant the potion with the power of your intent. You could use these potions when you have specific needs, or you could use one or more of them on a regular basis to maintain positive conditions in your life. As with all magick, the more energy and effort that you put into a spell, the better the result that you will obtain from it.

Whenever possible in making and drinking these potions, do use your finest china, your best table linens, your good silverware, and so on. If you use the potions regularly, make a small ceremony of their preparation. Such rituals are comforting. They center you and make life more meaningful. Rituals also encourage the flow of magick through you and throughout your life.

Recipes for many different potions are given here. They are all meant to be made by you for yourself. It is unethical to administer a potion to someone without that person's knowledge and informed consent. To violate someone in that way is to invite negative repercussions to rebound upon you, so you definitely don't want to start brewing up potions and serving them to people who have no idea what they are drinking.

Each of these potions is designed to draw specific positive energies toward you. You can prepare them however you usually make tea, such as with milk and sugar. Be sure to only stir them deosil though, because you are working to attract those vibrations that will help you to achieve your objective. Some of the potions call for symbols such as hearts and runes to be stirred into them. First stir those potions deosil, then stir the shape of the symbol into them. It's fine if you would prefer to use an alternate symbol, such as a different rune. Be sure to focus on your magickal objective while you drink the potions.

The Spell

A potion spell, like any other spell, begins when you first think about making it. The next step is to gather everything that you need to make the potion. As you do this, focus your magickal attention on the effect that you want your potion to have. Visualize the changes that you would like the potion to manifest in you and in the circumstances of your life.

Get into a magickal mood when you are ready to make the potion. Create sacred space in the place where you will make it and in the place where you will drink it. Empty your kettle of any standing water, and fill it with fresh water. Heat the kettle until the water is at a full boil, with steam pouring from the spout. Regard the boiling kettle and say:

Powers of Water, Powers of Fire,
Bring to me what I desire.

Put the herbs in the pot, or the tea bag(s) into the cup, and pour the boiling water over them. Allow the brew to steep for a bit. Inhale its steam, and say:

Powers of Earth, Powers of Air,
Draw to me all that is fair.

Remove the tea bag(s), or pour the tea from the pot into a cup. Raise power. Hold your hands over the cup for a moment, as you focus on infusing the potion with your magickal intent. This is the most important part of the spell, so use full power and give it your complete attention. Stir the tea and say:

This cup of tea is now enchanted,
with seeds of _____,[3] firmly planted.
Aromatic magickal potion,
As I drink, set my spell in motion.

Ingredients

water: Ordinary tap water is fine, but spring water or filtered water is preferable. If you become very interested in making tea potions, you may want to begin collecting water from natural sources, such as rain water, melted snow, or water from wells, streams, or springs to use in your potions. If you do this, be sure to only use water that you are certain is safe to drink.

---

3. Fill in the word or phrase, such as "peace" or "good health," that sums up your desire.

tea: When black tea is specified, it means ordinary tea, such as orange pekoe. Lemon balm tea means *Melissa officinalis*, which is also simply called balm. Ginger tea means tea that is brewed from a piece of freshly peeled ginger root; cinnamon tea means tea that is brewed from cinnamon sticks or chips. Rose tea means tea that is made from rose petals, rose hips, or a combination of the two. When a potion calls for more than one kind of tea, you can use two tea bags in the cup, or a spoonful of each herb, per cup of tea, in the pot.

You may find it easier to obtain commercial tea products, such as cinnamon tea or ginger tea. If so, try to use those products that contain natural ingredients. Dong quai, cat's claw, eyebright, feverfew, scullcap, uva ursi . . . there are esoteric herbs that can be used in tea potions, but this book's recipes focus on ingredients that are generally readily available in grocery stores.

sweetener: Honey has the magickal power of attraction, so it is the ideal sweetener to use in tea potions. Ginger has many magickal qualities, so pieces of candied ginger also make good sweeteners for the potions. You could also use sugar, or no sweetener at all. Artificial sweeteners have no magick in them, but you can use them if you need to.

citrus: Lemon has the magickal powers of repelling and averting, so it is best not to use lemon in any of these potions unless it is listed as an ingredient. When lemon is called for, that is because it has a magickal correspondence with the potion's intent. In that case you can use a strip of lemon peel or a squeeze of fresh lemon juice. When the peel of any citrus fruit is called for, it means the zest, the colorful outer part of the skin of the fruit. Citrus peel may be used fresh or dried. Milk should not be added to potions that contain citrus, because it is likely to curdle.

other ingredients: When a potion calls for a crystal or other stone, you place it in the cup with the tea, but you DO NOT INGEST IT! You wash the stone after you drink the tea, and reserve it for future use. When a potion requires a cinnamon stick, you use it to stir the tea, then discard it after drinking the potion.

The Potions

Taste is individual, so it is unlikely that you will care for all of these potions. Do not use a potion whose taste you really dislike or one that contains an ingredient you are allergic to. Wherever possible, more than one recipe is given. Feel free to experiment, and create your own potions.

⚘ Abundance Potion ⚘

To encourage an abundance of good things in your life.

Black tea, with a strip of orange peel.

⚘ Beauty Potion ⚘

For males or females, to help you to feel good about your appearance; to encourage others to find you attractive.

Jasmine tea and hibiscus tea.

Note: Bathe your face in the steam from the cup before you drink the potion.

⁓ Clarity Potions ⁓

To encourage yourself to think clearly; to help you to read people and situations correctly.

Black tea, with a squeeze of fresh lemon.
Spearmint tea, with a strip of tangerine peel.
Peppermint tea, with a clear quartz crystal.

Optional: a clear glass cup or mug

⁓ Courage Potion ⁓

To help you to feel more courageous; to help you to face things bravely.

Black tea, with a piece of freshly peeled ginger root, or several pieces of candied ginger.

Optional: a mug with a lion or a wolf on it

⁓ Creativity Potion ⁓

To activate your creative powers. When you stir the potion, stir the shape of this rune into it: ᚲ

Chamomile tea and peppermint tea, with three cardamom pods.

Note: Discard the cardamom pods after you drink the potion.

⁓ Friendship Potion ⁓

To encourage new friends to enter your life; to encourage new friendships to blossom; to encourage good relationships with your friends; to encourage a friendlier personality in yourself. When you stir the potion, stir the shape of this rune into it: ᛗ

Strawberry leaf tea, with a rose quartz.

⚘ Good Health Potions ⚘

To help your body to maintain its good health. When you stir these potions, stir the shape of the ankh into them: ☥

Yerba maté tea, with a slice of dried apple.
Ginger tea and rose hip tea, with a slice of dried apple.

Note: Eat the dried apple after the tea is finished.

Green tea and peppermint tea.
Green tea and ginseng tea.
Green tea and rose hip tea.

Optional: a green cup or mug

⚘ Good Luck Potion ⚘

To attract good luck; to encourage lucky breaks. When you stir the potion, stir the shape of this rune into it: ᚺ

Peppermint tea and dill seed tea, with a star anise.

Note: Discard the dill seeds and the star anise after you drink the tea. You could also wash the star anise, dry it, and retain it as a good luck charm. This potion is best drunk from your favorite cup or mug.

⚘ Happiness Potions ⚘

To encourage contentment; to help you to focus on your blessings, rather than on your problems. When you stir these potions, stir the shape of this rune into them: ᛗ

Note: These potions will not treat depression. That is a medical condition which requires medical treatment.

Earl Grey tea, with lemon.
Black tea, with a strip of tangerine peel.
Lemon balm tea, with a slice of dried apple.

Note: If you use the lemon balm tea, eat the dried apple after you drink the potion.

Good Marriage Potion

To encourage a happy, contented relationship. When you stir the potion, stir the shape of this rune into it: ᚷ
Note: This potion will not stop abuse or solve other serious problems. Those require help from professionals or the legal system.

Red clover tea and linden flower tea and a small clear quartz crystal.

Note: This potions is best drunk by both spouses, together.

Meditation Potion

To encourage a meditative state of mind. When you stir this potion, stir the shape of this rune into it: ᚦ

Chamomile tea, with a pinch of aniseed.

Optional: a cup that is any shade of blue or purple

Note: Discard the aniseed after the tea has finished steeping.

Peace Potion

To encourage inner peace; to encourage peaceful relationships with others; to encourage peaceful conditions around you.

Note: This potion will not stop violence or end abuse. You need to call the police for that.

Chamomile tea and hibiscus tea, with a small blue stone or a small rose quartz.

Note: This potion can be made at home and taken in a thermos to the place where peace is sought, such as work or school.

↲ Personal Power Potion ↝

To empower you; to increase your awareness of your powers; to help you to develop your personal powers; to strengthen your personal powers; to help you to learn (or remember) that "power with" is better than "power over"; to encourage you to use your powers wisely. When you stir the potion, stir the shape of this rune into it: ⟩

Ginseng tea and a small quartz crystal, stirred eight times with a cinnamon stick.

Optional: an orange or magenta cup, or a mug that has a picture of your power animal or the symbol for your astrological sign on it

↲ Psychism Potion ↝

To activate your psychic gifts; to encourage the development of your psychic abilities; to prepare you for divination, such as casting runes or scrying. When you stir the potion, stir the shape of this rune into it: ᚠ

Peppermint tea and rose tea, with a small piece of mastic resin.

Optional: To increase its potency, burn patchouli incense or mastic resin while you drink this potion. (Mastic resin, also called gum mastic, should be burned over self-igniting charcoal. It can be found in Middle Eastern grocery shops.)

Spirituality Potions

To awaken your spirituality; to encourage your spiritual development. When you stir the potion, stir the shape of this rune into it: ᛒ

Jasmine tea, with a few drops of passionflower juice.
Green tea, with five juniper berries.

Optional: a white, violet, or light blue cup

Note: Do not eat the juniper berries, which can be found where gourmet spices are sold. Discard them after you finish the tea, or wash them, dry them thoroughly, and retain them as charms.

Success Potions

To encourage success in your life, in your career, or in any specific endeavor. When you stir these potions, stir the shapes of these three runes into them: ᛏ ᚹ ᛊ

Lemon balm tea, with one dried allspice berry.
Cinnamon tea, with a scant drop of pure vanilla extract.
Ginger tea, with a cinnamon stick and a strip of orange peel.

Optional: a golden spoon to stir the potion; an orange cup or mug

Note: Do not eat the allspice berry (a type of pepper found where spices are sold). Discard it after you finish the potion, or wash it, dry it thoroughly, and retain it as a charm.

Love Potions

Remember that it is ethical to invite love into your life, but not ethical to use magick to try to force someone to love you. The Goddess of Love often has a cruel sense of humor, so don't tempt her by misusing love spells or potions.

⁓ Love-Drawing Potions ⁓

To attract love; to make yourself receptive to love. When you stir these potions, stir the shape of this rune into them: X

> Peppermint tea and rose hip tea.
> Lemon balm tea and rose tea.
> Strawberry leaf tea and lemon balm tea.
> Jasmine tea, with one scant drop of pure vanilla extract.
> Black tea, with a cinnamon stick and a small rose quartz.
>
> *Optional*: a pink or orange cup or mug

⁓ Surrounded by Love Potion ⁓

To encourage you to recognize and appreciate the love that is already in your life. When you stir this potion, stir the shape of a heart into it.

> At least two of the following: hibiscus tea, strawberry leaf tea, raspberry leaf tea, rose hip tea, plus a slice of dried apple.
>
> *Optional*: a rose-pink cup or mug

Note: Put the dried apple into the cup before you add the boiling water and eat it after the potion is finished.

⁓ Open to Love Potion ⁓

To encourage you to learn to accept the love that is all around you.

Lemon balm tea and rose tea, with a small rose quartz. Linden flower tea, with a cinnamon stick and a freshwater pearl.

Optional: a clear glass cup or mug

⁓ Self-Love Potion ⁓

To encourage you to learn to love and appreciate yourself. When you stir this potion, stir the shape of a heart into it.

Earl Grey tea, with a cinnamon stick and a small rose quartz.

Optional: a pink cup or mug

⁓ True Love Potion ⁓

To help you to recognize and be receptive to your true love, when he or she enters your life.

Jasmine tea, with one needle of fresh or dried rosemary.

⁓ Return Potion ⁓

To request the return of a lover. When you stir the potion, stir the shape of this rune into it: ᚱ

Note: Use this spell as an invitation, not a command. Read the instructions for the "Come Back to Me Spell" on page 50, and remember that it is not ethical to use magick to try to force someone to get back together with you.

Black tea, with honey and a piece of dried pineapple.

Note: Put the pineapple in the cup with the tea, and eat it after the tea is finished.

Money Potions

Money potions are not substitutes for steady effort or gainful employment. You have to work in order for these potions to work.

⚘ Money-Drawing Potions ⚘

To attract monetary gain; to encourage financial stability. When you stir these potions, stir the shape of this rune into them: ᚠ

Chamomile tea and blackberry leaf tea.

Clover tea and mint tea, with three sunflower seeds.

Note: If the seeds have shells, discard them after you drink the potion; if they are unshelled, eat them afterward.

Ginger tea, with four cloves and a strip of orange peel.

Note: Discard the cloves and orange peel after you drink the potion.

Mint tea, with three poppy seeds and a small green stone, such as aventurine.

Note: Discard the poppy seeds, but wash and retain the aventurine after drinking the potion.

Clover tea and chamomile tea, with an almond.

Optional: a green cup or mug; a golden spoon to stir the tea; honey to sweeten the potion

Note: Eat the almond after you drink the potion.

⋊ Prosperity Potions ⋉

To encourage financial abundance and material gain. When you stir these potions, stir the shape of this rune into them: ᚠ

>Earl Grey tea, with one saffron thread.
>Mint tea, with a strip of orange peel and a small green stone, such as aventurine.

>*Optional*: a sterling silver spoon, to stir the tea

Note: Discard the orange peel, but wash and retain the stone after drinking the potion.

Sex Magick Potions

⋊ Female Potions ⋉

To enhance female energy, sexuality, and sexual energy. When you stir these potions, stir the shape of this symbol into them: ♀

>Damiana tea and rose tea or raspberry leaf tea, with a slice of dried pear.
>Saw palmetto tea and damiana tea, with a slice of dried pear. (Health food stores carry these teas.)

Note: Eat the pear after the tea is finished.

⋊ Male Potions ⋉

To enhance male energy, sexuality, and sexual energy. When you stir these potions, stir the shape of this symbol into them: ♂

>Ginseng tea and ginger tea, with a cinnamon stick.
>Yerba maté and yohimbine tea, with five coriander seeds.

Note: Discard the coriander after the tea is finished.

⚘ Desire Potion ⚘

For males and females, to encourage you to feel desirable; to encourage others to feel desire for you. When you stir this potion, stir the shape of this rune into it: ◊

> Jasmine tea, with rose hips or rose hip tea.

Note: Discard the rose hips after the tea is finished. You could also rinse them, dry them thoroughly, and keep them with you as charms.

⚘ Lust Potions ⚘

For males and females, to activate your sexual energy. When you stir these potions, stir the shape of this rune into them: ᚾ

> Ginger tea and dill seed tea.
> Ginseng tea and yerba maté tea.
> Hibiscus tea, with a pinch of celery seed.

Optional: a mug with a picture of a wolf or a goat on it

Sleep and Dreams Potions

These potions are best drunk at bedtime.

⚘ Peaceful Sleep Potions ⚘

To facilitate a good night's sleep.

> Chamomile tea and linden flower tea, with five poppy seeds.
> Valerian tea and linden flower tea.

Optional: a blue cup or mug

⁓ Pleasant Dreams Potions ⁓

To encourage restful sleep and pleasant dreams.

Chamomile tea and spearmint tea.
Chamomile tea and valerian tea.
Spearmint tea and valerian tea.

Optional: a pale blue cup

Glossary

Glossary of Deity Names

Bast isn't just a cat goddess. Hermes is far more complex than a simple messenger god. Ma'at has dominion over truth, justice, and many other things beside social order. The Afro-Caribbean deities are more properly called loas and orishas in the New World. Parvati is an aspect of Kali, whom some consider an aspect of Durga. Most of the stories you know about the Greco-Roman deities are late myths, patriarchal ones that obscure, diminish, or subvert the true nature of the various goddesses. . . . There is a great deal more to these deities than this book has room to tell, but the following list will give a basic idea of who they are. Selket, Selkhet, Selkit, Selqet—their names have many variations, and can be spelled in different ways. For this book, I have used the spellings that seem to me to be the easiest to pronounce.

DEITY	TRADITION	ATTRIBUTE
Abeona	Roman	Goddess of children
Abundantia	Roman	Goddess of abundance
Acca Larentia	Etruscan	Earth goddess
Adeona	Roman	Goddess of schoolchildren
Aega	Greek	Solar goddess
Aeolus	Greek	Wind god
Aerten	Celtic	Goddess of fate
Aine	Irish	Lunar goddess
Allat	Arabian	Great Goddess; Earth Mother
Amor	Roman	Love god
Anahita	Persian	Great Goddess of waters
Anath	Semitic	Great Goddess of love and war
Anatha Baetyl	Semitic	A title of Anath
Andarta	Romano-Celtic	Mother goddess
Anesidora	Greek	A title of Pandora
Angus	Celtic	God of love and youth

Aphrodite	Greek	Goddess of love
Apollo	Greek	Sun god
Aquilo	Roman	God of the North Wind
Artemis	Greek	Lunar goddess
Atalanta	Greek	Goddess of the hunt
Atargatis	Semitic	Love goddess
Athene	Greek	Goddess of wisdom
Aya	Mesopotamian	Dawn goddess
Baal	Middle Eastern	Sky Father
Baldur	Norse	God of light
Bast	Egyptian	Cat goddess
Benzaiten	Japanese	Goddess of love and happiness
Bes	Egyptian	Guardian god
Blathnat	Celtic	Goddess of flowers
Brigid	Celtic	Great Goddess; Triple Goddess
Britomartis	Cretan	Lunar goddess
Canola	Irish	Harp goddess
Cardea	Roman	White Goddess
Catheña	Mojave Indian	Goddess of love
Cernunnos	Celtic	Horned God
Cerridwen	Celtic	White Goddess
Changing Woman	Navajo Indian	Earth and sky goddess
Chantico	Aztec	Hearth goddess
Chie	Chibcha Indian	Goddess of fun and happiness
Cliodna	Celtic	Goddess of beauty
Concordia	Roman	Goddess of good relations
Copia	Roman	Goddess of plenty
Copper Woman	Pacific Northwest Indian	Goddess of wealth
Cybele	Near Eastern	Great Mother Goddess
Cytherea	Greek	Epithet for Venus or Aphrodite
The Dagda	Celtic	Father god
Damona	Celtic	Goddess of domestic animals
Danu	Celtic	Universal mother goddess

Dazimus	Sumerian	Goddess of healing
Demeter	Greek	Earth Mother
Deohako	Seneca Indian	Vegetation goddess
Deverra	Roman	Goddess of new mothers
Diana	Roman	Triple lunar goddess
Diana Triformis	Roman	Title, The Three Dianas
Dictynna	Cretan	A title of Britomartis
Dike	Greek	Goddess of justice
Dolya	Slavic	Goddess of fate
Durga	Hindu	Great Goddess
Eir	Norse	Goddess of mercy and healing
Eirene	Greek	Goddess of peace
Eos	Greek	Goddess of daybreak
Epona	Romano-Celtic	Horse goddess
Ertha	Germanic	Earth Mother
Erzulie	Afro-Caribbean	Love goddess aspect of Oshun
Esmerelda	Incan	Goddess of love and emeralds
Fana	Etruscan	Earth goddess
Feng Po	Chinese	Wind god/goddess
Forseti	Norse	God of justice and mediation
Freya	Norse	Great Goddess
Frigg	Germanic	Great Goddess
Fulla	Norse	Mother goddess
Fura-Chogue	Colombian	Mother goddess
Gaia	Greek	Mother Earth
Gefion	Norse	Goddess of maidens
Gerd	Norse	Earth Mother
Geshtinanna	Sumerian	Goddess of the power in grapes
Glispa	Navajo Indian	Goddess of healing
Goda	Norse	Love-and-death goddess
Gonlod	Norse	Goddess of poetry
The Graces	Greek	Goddesses of gracefulness
Gula	Babylonian	Mother goddess
Habondia	Germano-Celtic	Harvest and fertility goddess

Hades	Greek	Underworld god
Hanwi	Plains Indian	Grandmother Moon
Hathor	Egyptian	Great Mother Goddess
Hecate	Greek	Triple lunar goddess
Heimdall	Norse	Guardian and creator god
Helios	Greek	Sun god
Hera	Greek	Great Goddess
Hermes	Greek	Messenger god
The Hesperides	Greek	Multiple lunar goddess
Hestia	Greek	Hearth goddess
Hlin	Norse	Goddess of consolation
Holda	Germanic	Love-and-death goddess
Hygeia	Greek	Goddess of healing
Inanna	Sumerian	Great Goddess of love and war
Intercidona	Roman	Goddess of infants
Ishhara	Babylonian	Goddess of love
Ishtar	Sumerian	Great Mother goddess
Isis	Egyptian	Universal mother goddess
Jana	Roman	Lunar goddess
Janus	Roman	God of beginnings and endings
Jara	Hindu	Household goddess
Jezanna	Zimbabwean	Lunar goddess
Juno	Roman	Goddess of women
Juno Lucina	Roman	An aspect of Juno
Jupiter	Roman	Sky Father
Jupiter Victor	Roman	A title of Jupiter
Kadi	Assyrian	Goddess of justice
Khonsu	Egyptian	Lunar god
Kwan Yin	Chinese	Goddess of compassion
Lada	Slavic	Goddess of love
Lady of the Lake	Celtic	Sovereignty goddess
Laima	Lithuanian	Goddess of fate
Lakshmi	Hindu	Goddess of love and wealth
The Lares	Roman	Guardian deities
La Sirene	Afro-Caribbean	Sea goddess aspect of Erzulie

Legba	Afro-Caribbean	Messenger god
Liber	Roman	Fertility god
Lucina	Roman	Goddess of celestial light
Ma'at	Egyptian	Goddess of social order
Maeve	Irish	Sovereignty goddess
Maha Lakshmi	Hindu	Title, Great Lakshmi
Maia	Greco-Roman	Goddess of Spring
Marduk	Babylonian	God of order and civilization
Mars Ollodius	Romano-Celtic	God of peaceful protection
Maximón	Guatemalan	Death and fertility god
Mercury	Roman	Messenger god
Milda	Lithuanian	Goddess of love
Minerva	Roman	Goddess of wisdom and war
The Morrigan	Celtic	Great Goddess; war goddess
The Muses	Greek	Goddesses of inspiration
Nantosuelta	Celtic	Water goddess
Nehalennia	Germanic	Goddess of seafaring
Neith	Egyptian	Great Goddess; astral goddess
Nephthys	Egyptian	Death goddess
Neptune	Roman	Sea god
Nike	Greek	Goddess of victory
Nikkal	Canaanite	Goddess of fruit
Nimuë	Welsh	Goddess of enchantment
Niorun	Norse	Goddess of dreams
Njord	Norse	Wind and sea god
Obatala	Afro-Caribbean	Sky Father
Odin	Norse/Germanic	Sky Father
Ogun	Afro-Caribbean	God of smithcraft
Olwen	Celtic	Flower goddess
Oshun	Afro-Caribbean	Goddess of love and sensuality
Osiris	Egyptian	God of rebirth
Ostara	Saxon	Goddess of Spring
Otter Woman	Cood Indian	Water goddess
Pachamama	Incan	Earth goddess

Pandora	Greek	Goddess of blessings
Parvati	Hindu	Fertility goddess
The Penates	Roman	Household gods
Persephone	Greek	Maiden goddess
Philotes	Greek	Goddess of affection
Pietas	Roman	Goddess of duty
Pilumnus	Roman	God who guards infants
Pluto	Roman	Underworld god
Potnia	Greco-Roman	Goddess of weaving
Ra	Egyptian	Sun god; head of the pantheon
Renenutet	Egyptian	Goddess of fortune
Rhea	Greek	Earth goddess
Rhiannon	Celtic	Horse goddess
Rosmerta	Romano-Celtic	Goddess of plenty
Salmon Woman	Samish Indian	Sea goddess
Sarah	Middle Eastern	Earth goddess
Sasthi	Hindu	Goddess of children
Saturn	Roman	God of time
Sekhmet	Egyptian	Solar goddess
Selket	Egyptian	Scorpion goddess
Sesheta	Egyptian	Goddess of record-keeping
The Seven Hathors	Egyptian	Birth goddesses
Shamash	Babylonian	Sun god
Shekinah	Hebrew	Goddess of wisdom
Sigyn	Norse	Earthquake goddess
Sjofna	Norse	Goddess of passion
Skan	Lakota Indian	Spirit of motion
Stribog	Slavic	God of winds
Sulis	Romano-Celtic	Goddess of healing springs
Syria Dea	Near Eastern	Great Goddess
Tana	Etruscan	Star goddess
Thor	Norse	Thunder god
Thoth	Egyptian	God of wisdom and magick
Tlaloc	Olmec/Aztec	Rain god
Tonantzin	Aztec	Birth goddess
Tsao-Chün	Chinese	Hearth god

Tyr	Norse	God of war and justice
Ukat	Yana Indian	Goddess of good luck
Ushas	Hindu	Dawn goddess
Vara	Norse	Goddess of love
Venus	Roman	Goddess of love
Verplace	Roman	Goddess of domestic harmony
Vesta	Roman	Hearth goddess
Volumna	Roman	Nursery goddess
Xochiquetzal	Aztec	Flower goddess
Yemaya	Afro-Caribbean	Ocean Mother
Zemlya	Slavic	Earth Mother
Zeus	Greek	Sky Father
The Zorya	Slavic	Triple goddess of dawn, sunset, midnight

Other Deities

Great Goddess: A powerful, influential goddess who has many aspects, dominion over diverse things, and/or a long tradition of widespread worship. Great Goddesses are often mother goddesses and the chief goddesses of their pantheon.

Khmara: Chimera; phantasm; dark dream; cloud torture; Ukrainian word for cloud. The name Mara refers to both the sea and to the night. In different cultures Mara (known by that and other related names, such as Marena Moru and the Morrigan) has variously been a goddess of death, bitterness, evil, sickness, ruin, darkness, and night. The word "mara," or "mare" (as in "nightmare"), and its related forms have also been used in several cultures for malevolent spirits or entities who smother sleeping human beings or inflict pain, bad dreams, delirium, sickness, or death upon them.

The Kikimora: Slavic household spirits

The Lady: The Goddess. Whether called the Goddess, the Great Goddess, or by any of her many individual names, she is the prime deity of witches.

The Lord: The God. Also known by many individual names, he is the partner of the Goddess. In various cultures he is considered her son or her consort.

Lords of the Watchtowers: Deities of the cardinal points.

Ocean Mother: A mother goddess who has dominion over the sea. Ocean Mothers are often depicted wearing pearls and blue robes.

Sky Father: A powerful father god. Usually the chief deity of his pantheon, he is often considered the creator. Sky

Fathers generally have dominion over the weather, especially thunder and lightning.

Triple Goddess: A goddess with three aspects, often those of Maiden, Mother, and Crone or of the lunar phases.

White Goddess: A goddess of life and death. White Goddesses are often associated with mills, where grain is ground (killed) to produce flour that will provide bread (life).

Index

~Index of Spells~